The Path of Joy

To Sarah,
So great meeting
you! May the
words of this
book lead you
into greater intimacy
with the Lord!
Warmly,
Marnie

Other Books From Leadership Resources

Pursuing God
Naked and Unashamed
Changed
Unlikely Warriors
Friendly Fire
A Quiet Heart

The Language of the Heart
Beyond Independence
Shoulder to Shoulder
Finishing Well in Life and Ministry
Adequate!

Inductive Bible Study Series
  Proverbs: Lessons for the Growing Years (Jr/Sr High)
  Inductive Bible Study Handbook
  Inductive Bible Study Books: Jonah, Philippians, Ruth

A Servant Series
  Marriage, Parenting and Forgiveness
  Reconciliation, Fellowship and the Grace of God

The Path of JOY

Enjoying Intimacy With God

MARNIE CARLSON

Leadership Resources International
Palos Heights • Illinois

Published by LEADERSHIP RESOURCES INTERNATIONAL
12575 Ridgeland Ave., Palos Heights, IL 60463

THE PATH OF JOY

Cover design: Kathy Burrows
Cover photograph: Marnie Carlson
ISBN 0-9709482-0-4

CONTENTS

Dedicated to my husband,
Dean,
who has encouraged and
supported me along
the path of joy

A CHILDLIKE JOY

When our son, Aaron, was about four years old, he liked to bring me "gifts" from our backyard. One day he ran into the house shouting, "Mommy, look what I have for you!"

From behind his back he revealed two clenched fists. My gift wasn't hard to spot. Jagged pieces of grass peeked out from between his chubby fingers. (Aaron usually picked me dandelion bouquets, but on those occasions when our yard wasn't sprouting his favorite yellow flower, I received a bouquet of grass instead.)

"Thank you, Aaron, for the beautiful grass!" Reaching down, I scooped him into my arms and whispered in his ear, "Let's put it in some water." Aaron nodded eagerly.

I carried him to the counter and set him down. Then I filled a cup with water, and Aaron carefully dropped in the grass one blade at a time. We placed the cup near the kitchen sink, so I would have plenty of opportunities to admire my present.

Later that day as I passed through the kitchen, I paused by the cup and thought about the pleasure the grass gave Aaron. My son's delight over a handful of grass caused me to stop and consider my relationship with God. If Aaron could have such tremendous appreciation for something as ordinary as grass, what kind of pleasure and appreciation should I have in God?

On that summer day years ago, I asked myself some questions: *Do I find my greatest joy in God? Do I experience the child-like pleasure of simply delighting in Him throughout my day? When I get up in the morning, are my waking thoughts about God?*

When we look at the prophet, Jeremiah, we find that his first thoughts of the day were centered on God. Referring to the Lord's great mercy and compassion, Jeremiah said, "They are new every morning; great is your faithfulness" (Lam. 3:23). Jeremiah made this statement regarding God's faithfulness while he was experiencing terrible afflictions. In the midst of intense trials, Jeremiah affirmed God's unfailing love. Jeremiah anticipated God's faithfulness and compassion from one morning to the next.

Inspired by Jeremiah's praise for the Lord, Thomas Chisholm penned the words to the hymn *Great Is Thy Faithfulness*:

> Great is Thy faithfulness, O God my Father,
> There is no shadow of turning with Thee;
> Thou changest not, Thy compassions they fail not;
> As Thou hast been Thou forever wilt be.
> Great is Thy faithfulness! Great is Thy faithfulness!
> Morning by morning new mercies I see;
> All I have needed Thy hand hath provided,
> Great is Thy faithfulness, Lord unto me![1]

"All I have needed Thy hand hath provided," wrote Chisholm. I wonder if we believe God has provided all we need. In the depths of our souls, are we satisfied with Him? Do you and I find our deepest joy in the Lord?

When we look at the pages of Scripture for examples of people who found their joy in God, we discover in the book of Acts that the early Christians rejoiced in God as a way of life. The believers at the church in Jerusalem are described as having "glad and sincere hearts, praising God and enjoying the favor of all the people" (Acts 2:46,47).

As we think about these first Christians who experienced great joy, we might say, "The church was getting started then, so that's why the people were rejoicing. But that was a long time ago. Things are different now." Consequently, we relegate joy to the archives of a bygone era.

What happened?

Somehow life became complicated. Our busy schedules and relentless pressures have dulled our senses to the Lord. His mercies may be new each morning, but so are rush hour traffic, housework, errands, classes, appointments, and deadlines. Added to this, is the tremendous instability in the world that encroaches on our personal world.

Deep inside us we feel a gnawing. A churning. In our hearts we yearn for a deep, satisfying relationship of joy with the Lord. But we don't know what to do. Perhaps that is our problem. We are so busy doing, we have forgotten that being a Christian is having a relationship of love with Jesus Christ.

Although Revelation 3:20 is often used as an evangelistic verse, in this verse Jesus is pictured as seeking entrance into His own church. In this portion of Scripture, we see the relationship Jesus desires to have with all who hear His voice and respond to

His call. Jesus said, "Here I am! I stand at the door and knock. If anyone hears my voice and opens the door, I will come in and eat with him, and he with me."

Think of a time, maybe an anniversary or some other special occasion, when you enjoyed the company of another person over a leisurely meal. This is a picture of the intimate relationship of love Jesus invites you and me to enjoy with Him. Of all the ways Jesus could have described the relationship He desires with us, He chose to compare it to the pleasure of enjoying an intimate dinner with someone we love.

The thought of enjoying this kind of relationship with Jesus may be difficult for some of us to comprehend. Few families sit down together for a meal anymore. Many of us grab fast food on the run or cook a frozen dinner in the microwave and eat it in front of the television. We have lost our ability to relate to others—even those closest to us—in deep, meaningful ways.

Our microwave mentality has found its way into our relationship with the Lord. We view our relationship with Him like the drive-through at a fast food restaurant. We place our prayer order, grab thirty seconds of devotions, and speed away.

We settle for convenience over knowledge. Feelings over truth. Surface over depth. We stuff ourselves with fast food, yet we remain hungry and dissatisfied.

Are you tired of trying to satisfy the hunger of your soul with fast food? Listen to Jesus' words a second time: "Here I am! I stand at the door and knock. If anyone hears my voice and opens the door, I will come in and eat with him, and he with me" (Rev. 3:20).

If you hear His voice, listen to what He is saying. Jesus is extending to you His gracious invitation to know Him...to enjoy Him...to long for Him...to be satisfied with Him. This is the path of joy. Jesus is calling you to walk with Him along this path in the pleasure of His company.

As we proceed through this book, *The Path of Joy*, think of the chapters like stepping-stones that wind through a garden. Just as stepping-stones have different shapes, so these chapters have different shapes. Each chapter looks at joy from a different point-of-view. The path of joy doesn't end with the final chapter of this book because joy has no end. This path leads us right into the presence of Jesus where we will enjoy intimacy with Him forever.

Do you long to experience the joy of an intimate relationship with Jesus? Would you like to enjoy the childlike wonder of discovering Him afresh each day? Join me in pursuing a satisfying relationship of love with Jesus Christ on the path of joy.

You have made known to me the path of life;
you will fill me with joy in your presence,
with eternal pleasures at your right hand
(Psalm 16:11).

1

HAPPINESS AND JOY

A research company conducted a poll of nearly 1,000 teenagers to determine the one thing teens want most from life. Happiness won first place. The teenagers valued happiness more than:

a long life
marriage and family
financial success
career success
religious satisfaction
love
personal success
personal contribution to society
friends
health
education.[1]

If you could talk with these teenagers about what is most important in life, what would you tell them? What do you and I value most? What motivates us? If we are motivated by happiness, then we want to make sure it's a worthwhile goal.

Is it?

In this opening chapter, we will discover whether happiness and joy are the same or different. An understanding of happiness and joy will help us to see what we value most in life.

A POPULAR PURSUIT

While reading the *Chicago Tribune* one evening, I came across an article called "Search for Meaning" that described the American quest for happiness:

> Never before in history has a nation been endowed with the personal freedoms and material prosperity to engage so vigorously in the "pursuit of happiness" as we Americans...
>
> Yet for reasons that mystify many of our wisest pundits, millions of us are miserable. How else to explain the fact that depression in America now outnumbers all other medical symptoms combined?...Why are we so troubled and unhappy?[2]

The pursuit of happiness has become a popular topic. One day when I was at the library, I noticed several shelves filled with books on how to be happy. I was interested to see what the authors had to say, so I sat down at a table and began to read. That afternoon I read many opinions on how to be happy, but no one gave me anything concrete. Absolute.

With so many conflicting opinions on the definition of happiness and how to attain it, how could any one of them be true?

Although no one could give me absolute truth about how to be happy, there is no shortage of people who are willing to offer their advice.

If we turn on the talk shows, pick up a magazine, or glance at billboards, we discover a myriad of different opinions on how we can attain happiness. We need to take a vacation, drive the right car, buy the latest electronic gadget, get a raise, learn relaxation techniques, find a new house, find a new spouse, win the lottery.

Most people have bought into this dream of happiness. But does this dream have a happy ending, or is it only a dream? Is this the path to experiencing the fulfillment we long for?

God tells us about a path we probably won't hear about on a talk show. In the Psalms, we read: "You have made known to me the path of life; you will fill me with joy in your presence, with eternal pleasures at your right hand" (16:11).

Along the path of life we find joy, fulfillment, and eternal pleasures. Who wouldn't want this? We might assume most people would be scrambling to get on this path. This isn't the case. The path of life is narrow, and few people find it (Matt. 7:13-14). But it's not because the way to this path is hidden. God makes the way readily known to us in His Word. As we begin, let's ask God to show us if we are on the path of life.

In the Bible, the word *path* refers to a way of life, conduct, or thought. Our way of life is determined by our actions. Our actions are determined by our thoughts. Our thoughts are determined by our beliefs. Our beliefs determine the path we follow. You and I stand at the crossroad. What path will we pursue?

MY PURSUIT OF HAPPINESS

When I was in high school, I knew what path I wanted to pursue. Like the teens in the survey, happiness headed my list of priorities. I decided the best way to achieve my dream of happiness was to attend a great college and land an impressive job.

In the closet of my bedroom, I had several large grocery store boxes filled with college catalogs from schools all over the country. I used to stay up late at night and spend hours browsing through my catalogs. Lying in my bed, I surrounded myself with them. I envisioned myself attending a renowned school of my choice. I imagined myself graduating and beginning a prestigious career. I would achieve all of my dreams, have everything I wanted, and be happy.

Although I had great plans for my future happiness, my situation at the time was not so happy. Because of the instability in my family, I felt like I lived on a tight rope. I cautiously inched my way through life with the constant fear that at any moment I might fall. Then it happened.

I fell.

My dream for happiness crashed the day my father left home. Although he was vice president of an oil company, his departure meant I would not be able to attend my "dream" school.

I no longer stayed up late at night to read my catalogs. My visions of strolling along tree-lined boulevards on my way to class evaporated. My plans for happiness vanished.

After a few months, I reluctantly decided to part with my catalogs. I didn't like looking at them each day when I opened my closet. I woke up early one morning and dragged my dusty boxes to the end of the driveway. One-by-one, I dropped my treasured catalogs into the garbage can. I looked at them one last time, wiped my tears, and put the lid on the can.

Later that morning, I watched out the kitchen window as two men dumped my dream for happiness into a garbage truck and drove away. My dream for happiness went up in smoke. Literally. At a garbage dump.

That painful experience taught me a lesson I didn't want to learn: happiness is circumstantial. Things happened to me that I hadn't planned on. The map I had carefully charted for my life was obsolete. Circumstances in my life were beyond my ability to control. I discovered there is no such thing as lasting happiness.

SOLOMON'S SEARCH

Unlike my situation, in the book of 1 Kings we learn that King Solomon had everything he wanted and achieved all of his goals for happiness. "Solomon had four thousand stalls for chariot horses, and twelve thousand horses" (1 Kings 4:26). All of Solomon's goblets and household artifacts were made out of gold because silver was considered to be of little value (1 Kings 10:21).

If anyone would have recommended the pursuit of happiness as a worthwhile endeavor, it would have been Solomon. But is this what he suggested? We might be surprised by his answer. Listen to what Solomon said:

> I denied myself nothing my eyes desired; I refused my heart no pleasure. My heart took delight in all my work, and this was the reward for all my labor. Yet when I surveyed all that my hands had done and what I had toiled to achieve, *everything was meaningless, a chasing after the wind; nothing was gained under the sun* (Ecc. 2:10-11, emphasis added).

After giving his life to pursuing wealth, wives, and every imaginable pleasure, Solomon drew this wistful conclusion: "Meaningless! Meaningless!...Utterly meaningless! Everything is meaningless" (Ecc. 1:2). Although happiness is often seen as a worthwhile pursuit, Solomon said, "What does it accomplish?" (Ecc. 2:2 NASB).

King Solomon came to realize that the pursuit of happiness does not lead to a meaningful, satisfied life. It leads to discouragement and frustration. This is because happiness is based on favorable circumstances.

For instance, when the sun was shining and things looked bright for my future, I experienced a ray of happiness. But when my circumstances changed and the sun disappeared behind the clouds, my happiness also disappeared.

I discovered that the pursuit of happiness is a deception. A mirage. It's a popular, well-accepted illusion. Nevertheless, it cannot fulfill its promises. Happiness has the life span of a snowflake.

When I was a little girl, I used to run outside when I saw the first snowfall and try to catch snowflakes in my hand. But as soon as I caught a snowflake, the heat from my hand melted it. Disappointed at losing my snowflake, I caught another one. But it also melted. I found myself running to grab one snowflake after another until I was tired and out-of-breath.

Happiness is like a snowflake that lands on our hand. Happiness quickly melts in the heat of real life. Just when we think we are finally happy, our circumstances change and our happiness is gone. Just like chasing snowflakes, we keep pursuing happiness until we are tired and out-of-breath. Yet we keep running.

Haven't we all been disillusioned by something we thought would make us happy? Think of the various things that have made you happy—until your circumstances changed.

Do you and I want to base our lives on things that fall apart, wear out, get sick, die, rust, leave us, go out of style, or disappoint us in other ways? The path of happiness holds the promise of fulfillment, but reality proves its promise is hollow. Amazingly, many of us still continue along this path undeterred.

THE *IF ONLY* GAME

The way we pursue happiness is by trying to control our circumstances and other people. When we go through life trying to work all things together for our happiness, we are playing a game.

It's called the *If Only* game.

We won't find this game at any toy store. This is a fantasy game we play in our minds. We play this game by painting a mental picture of what we think will make us happy and then trying to figure out a way to make the fantasy a reality.

Satan, the originator of the *If Only* game, has kept it a bestseller since the beginning of time. Eve, the game's first player, fell victim to the fantasy of happiness when she believed Satan instead of God. Satan's strategy in his game with Eve was to plant questions in her mind about the reliability of God's Word and His care for her.

In Genesis 3:1-2, we see how Eve fell for Satan's game plan:

> Now the serpent was more crafty than any of the wild animals the LORD God had made. He said to the woman, "Did God really say, 'You must not eat from any tree in the garden'?" The woman said to the serpent, "We may eat fruit from the trees in the garden, but God did say, 'You must not eat fruit from the tree that is in the middle of the garden, and you must not touch it, or you will die.' "

Eve questioned whether she could trust God. We know this because she changed what God had said. In Genesis 1:17, God said not to *eat* from the tree, but she changed His words by adding the extra prohibition of not touching it. Apparently, she didn't consider His Word as binding, so she gave it her own slant.

Her doubt about God's wisdom showed she was having second thoughts about His love and care for her. Eve's suspicion about God created a false need in her. God loved Eve and was meeting every one of her needs. But she *imagined* He wasn't. When Eve believed Satan and mistrusted God, truth became obscured by Satan's illusion.

Eve felt she was lacking something that God hadn't provided. Satan reinforced her doubt and told Eve how to remedy the situation. Satan said, in effect, "Eve, *if only* you eat this fruit, you will become a god. This is your path to happiness! Don't let it pass you by!"

In Genesis 3:4-6, we read Satan's exact words to Eve:

> "You will not surely die," the serpent said to the woman. "For God knows that when you eat of it your eyes will be opened, and you will be like God, knowing good and evil." When the woman saw that the fruit of the tree was good for food and pleasing to the eye, and also desirable for gaining wisdom, she took some and ate it. She also gave some to her husband, who was with her, and he ate it.

Adam and Eve's path to happiness became the road to destruction. Tragically, they believed they were on the right path. In Proverbs, we read this warning: "There is a way that seems right to a man, but in the end it leads to death" (14:12). The path that looked so appealing and felt so right was, in fact, the way of death. Adam and Eve did not receive happiness. Instead, our first ancestors received fear, guilt, and death (Gen. 3:10-19).

Satan tempted Eve by getting her to imagine things that were not true. Satan's tactics have not changed over the years. He tempts you and me in the same way he tempted Eve. He creates illusions in our minds about what is true. Eve imagined she lacked something in God, so she looked for satisfaction apart from Him. If Satan can get us to *imagine* God isn't taking care of us, we become players in the *If Only* game.

HOW TO BECOME A PLAYER

Have you played the *If Only* game? Do you ever have thoughts like these?

If only my husband were more sensitive, then I'd be happy.
If only I had more money, then I'd be happy.
If only people would recognize all the work I do, then I'd be happy.

We don't play this deceptive game for long before we realize its built-in flaw: the if only's never end. Happiness evades us once again. When Satan lures us into his game, he doesn't reveal its devious hitch: this game has no winners.

What if your husband never changes?
What if you lose all your money?
What if no one ever thanks you for all your hard work?

How will you feel? The word *happy* will probably not be on your list of adjectives.

Happiness, in the *If Only* game, hinges on the fulfillment of a fantasy. When we make the fantasy of happiness our goal, we depend on our circumstances and how people respond to us for our sense of well-being and security. In our effort to hold onto happiness, we try to control everything and everyone. This is no simple task. Since circumstances and people are always changing, pursuing this course is like navigating a minefield. Those who walk this path live in misery.

I happened to meet a woman (I will call her Julie) who was

convinced that if she lost thirty pounds and moved out of her apartment to a house, then all of her problems would disappear and she would be happy. If Julie lost her weight and gained her house, would she be immune to the problems we all face?

In Julie's mind, yes. In reality, no. Julie was deceived by a fantasy. Her pursuit of happiness didn't bring her the happiness she sought. Instead, her distorted focus prevented her from enjoying all she had.

HOW TO QUIT THE GAME

How do we get off the merry-go-round of the pursuit of happiness? We need to discern truth from lies. God points us to His Word to find truth—not to our feelings and fantasies. Jesus said, "Your word is truth" (John 17:17). God's Word is the compass that guides us through life and provides the foundation of absolute truth.

If we don't depend on God's Word to guide us, our view of God, other people, and ourselves will be askew. It's like we're standing in the Leaning Tower of Pisa and wondering why everyone else is crooked!

When we make happiness our goal in life, we, like Julie, destine ourselves for discouragement. Happiness is an unworthy pursuit. A futile endeavor. A hopeless goal.

Is it wrong, then, for us to pursue our goals and desires? Not at all. For example, Julie's desire to lose weight and move out of her apartment was fine. The problem was, she made this desire her ultimate goal. She placed her sense of well-being in the hands of circumstances, instead of in the hands of God. When she didn't get what she wanted, when she wanted it, she became angry.

God has so much more for you and me than for us to waste our lives on futile pursuits. God tells us: "Delight yourself in the

LORD and he will give you the desires of your heart" (Ps. 37:4). We disentangle ourselves from the pursuit of happiness when we seek our delight in the unchanging God instead of our changing circumstances. As we delight in Him, He places *His* desires for us within our hearts.

Would you like to quit playing the *If Only* game? Are you willing to surrender to the Lord your life, your plans, your dreams, your goals—no matter what? How you answer that question will determine whether you quit playing the *If Only* game or if you go around the board one more time.

God doesn't want us spending our lives trying to work all things together for our happiness. He wants us to place our lives in His hands and trust Him to work all things together for His glory and our good. "God causes all things to work together for good to those who love God, to those who are called according to His purpose" (Rom. 8:28 NASB).

Through trusting in the sovereign Lord who controls all things, we are released from the grip of deceptive lies. We are free to experience the reality of everlasting joy, instead of the illusion of superficial happiness. We are free to enjoy an intimate relationship of love with Jesus Christ.

HAPPINESS AND JOY COMPARED

I once heard a man say, "I want my life filled with happiness and joy." We often hear people use the words *happiness* and *joy* interchangeably. But are these two words synonymous? Through a side-by-side comparison of happiness and joy, we will see what the Bible tells us.

Happiness	***Joy***
The *If Only* game showed us that happiness is elusive because it's based on favorable circumstances. Happiness is like cotton candy. It tastes good for a moment, but melts in our mouths before it reaches our stomachs. Happiness is momentary and fleeting. It's shallow, transitory nature renders it incapable of reaching our souls and satisfying us.	Biblical joy is not shallow and weak. It is deep-rooted and strong. The enduring quality of joy enables it to reach all the way down to our souls and fill us up with rich satisfaction. If happiness is cotton candy, then joy is a five-course meal! Jesus said, "That my joy may be in you, and that your joy may be made full" (John 15:11 NASB).
Happiness has the stability of a sand castle at high tide. Since happiness has no foundation, it collapses when the trials of life pound against it.	Joy is like a solid rock that rises majestically out of the water. The waves pound against it, but joy still stands. Joy is built on the solid rock of God. "Come, let us sing for joy to the LORD; let us shout aloud to the Rock of our salvation" (Ps. 95:1).
The pursuit of happiness is self-centered, and self is never satisfied.	Joy isn't centered on self. Joy is God-centered. "Then will I go...to God, my joy and my delight" (Ps. 43:4). "You have put gladness in my heart" (Ps. 4:7 NKJV). True, lasting joy originates in God and flows from God.

Those who aim for happiness must expend time, energy, and effort to try to produce happiness. It doesn't come easily and doesn't stay long. Happiness is something we grab when we get the chance.	We don't grab at joy. We receive it with open hands as God's gift to us. "God gives...joy" (Ecc. 2:26 NKJV). Joy isn't a product we work hard to produce. Joy is the by-product of resting in Jesus.
Happiness is a passing emotion—here today and gone tomorrow. We may feel happy right now, but that doesn't guarantee how we'll feel tomorrow.	Joy is not a fluctuating mood. Joy is from the Lord, and He never changes. Our joy is here today and here tomorrow! "No one will take away your joy" (John 16:22).

In his book, *Joy and Godliness*, John MacArthur offers this insight into the differences between happiness and joy:

> We live in a sad world—a world of despair, depression, unfulfillment, and dissatisfaction. Man defines happiness as an attitude of satisfaction and delight based upon circumstances. He relates happiness to happenings and happenstance. He regards it as something that can't be planned or programmed.
>
> Biblical joy, on the other hand, consists of the deep and abiding confidence that all is well, regardless of circumstances and difficulty. It is very different from worldly happiness. Biblical joy is always related to God and belongs only to those in Christ. It is the permanent possession of every believer—not a whimsical delight that comes and goes as chance offers opportunity.

> A good analogy of joy is this: it's the flag that flies on the castle of the heart when the King is in residence. Only Christians can know true and lasting joy. Christian joy is a gift from God to those who believe the gospel, produced in them by the Holy Spirit as they receive and obey the Word, mixed with trials with a hope set on future glory.[3]

SUPERNATURAL JOY

As we compare happiness and joy, I don't want to leave the impression that we should feel bad if we're happy! Many things in life cause us to feel happy. Like anyone else, I'd rather be happy than sad. I'm thankful to the Lord for all the happiness in my life.

For instance, one day I went shopping for a jacket. As I walked by a rack of clothes, I saw just the jacket I was looking for. But it was the only one left. I wondered if it would be my size. It was the right size, and it was on sale! When I took out my money at the cash register to pay for it, more money was deducted from the sale price. How do you think I felt? Happy! But doesn't everyone feel happy about finding a bargain?

Everyone, however, does not experience joy. Happiness is natural. Joy is supernatural.

Only those who have the Holy Spirit indwelling them are able to experience the supernatural joy the Holy Spirit gives. In Acts we read: "The disciples were filled with *joy and with the Holy Spirit*" (13:52 emphasis added). In the book of Romans, the Apostle Paul said, "For the kingdom of God is not a matter of eating and drinking, but of righteousness, peace and *joy in the Holy Spirit*." (14:17 emphasis added).

The basis of our joy is our fellowship with the Lord through His Spirit. The Apostle John wrote about our joy in fellowship with the Lord by saying, "And our fellowship is with the Father and with his Son, Jesus Christ. We write this to make our joy complete" (1 John 1:3-4).

God the Father has called us into fellowship—into an intimate relationship of love through His Son Jesus Christ. Since God is the source and giver of joy, the closer we walk with Him, the greater our joy. God nudges us into greater intimacy with Himself by continually revealing to us His love and faithfulness.

Joy is experienced within the context of a loving, trusting relationship with God. Love and trust are the foundation on which an intimate, enjoyable relationship with God is built. As strength and endurance are integral to a marathon runner, loving God and trusting Him are integral to experiencing a joyful relationship with Him. The joy we experience in fellowship with Jesus is far different from momentary happiness.

DOWN IS UP

God taught me the difference between happiness and joy through circumstances I would not have chosen. After I graduated from high school, I worked at a golf course and earned enough money to go away to college. (In the next chapter, I'll explain how God transformed my life while I was away at school.) My money ran out sooner than I expected, and I returned home.

While I lived at home, I cleaned houses and attended a college close to home. I never attended my "dream" school, but what I learned about God's love and sovereignty far surpassed my dreams. God took that dark alley in my life and turned it into a path of joy.

Cleaning houses left my mind free to think, and I began to think about God. I began to see that God's ways may not always be my ways, but His ways are always best.

God used my housecleaning job to accomplish a work in me that I wouldn't have anticipated. He used my job to strip off my veneer of happiness. Washing floors on my hands and knees was not part of the picture I had envisioned for myself. But as I scrubbed kitchen floors, I realized He was in the process of scrubbing away my pride. God was bringing me down rung-by-rung from my ivory tower.

I didn't keep my own bedroom clean. But I worked so hard at cleaning houses that my hands often cracked and bled from the eczema I developed. When the pain and swelling became so bad that I could hardly bend my fingers, I covered them with ointment and bandages and went to work.

I realize this may not sound like the path of joy. But God took a bad situation and turned it around for His glory and my good. Because He loved me, He didn't let me wander in my dream of happiness that could never bring me true joy. He graciously removed my circumstantial happiness so I would find my joy in Him. And I have. In Jesus, I have more than I would have ever dreamed possible.

UNCHANGING JOY

What are you trusting in for your security? Is it something that can change? If your security rests on something that can change, you can never rest securely. Your security is only as good as the object on which it rests.

You will never know lasting joy and peace unless you give yourself to something that is secure, solid, unchanging, and dependable. Jesus Christ is the only One who fits that description.

Jesus is the one constant in the universe who never changes. He is our solid rock, a dependable fortress that cannot be shaken. "He alone is my rock and my salvation; he is my fortress, I will never be shaken" (Ps. 62:2).

We have no guarantees for happiness in this world filled with tension and turmoil. But because Jesus doesn't change, He is able to guarantee us eternal security and joy—apart from our circumstances. "You have made known to me the path of life; you will fill me with joy in your presence, with eternal pleasures at your right hand" (Ps. 16:11).

When Jesus shows us the way to the path of life, He points to Himself. He is the narrow way, the only way. He is life and joy. Jesus said, "I am the way and the truth and the life. No one comes to the Father except through me" (John 14:6).

When our circumstances change, He is still the same. In our confusion, He is the way. In a world of lies, He is the truth. He gives us the spiritual life and joy we long for.

The path of joy *is* Jesus.

When we find our life in Him, we enter the path of joy and discover true satisfaction. What is hindering you from experiencing His life and joy? Give it all to Him. Walk closely with Jesus and enjoy the intimate relationship of love you were created for.

Responding to God's Word

1. What advice would you give to the teens in the survey who ranked happiness as their number one priority?

2. Have you played the *If Only* game in the past? What happened?

   Are you a current player? Complete the following sentence. I would be happy if only...

Would you like to quit the game? Are you willing to surrender to the Lord your life, your plans, your dreams, your goals—no matter what? Explain.

3. Eve imagined that God wasn't meeting her needs. How do doubts about God's love and care affect:

   Your relationship with Him

   Your ability to resist Satan

   Your joy

4. Describe how happiness and joy differ from one another. What do you find most interesting about these differences? How will knowing what these differences are help you to deal with a situation you are facing?

5. What dark alley in your life became a path of joy? How does Romans 8:28 help you with this?

What does Romans 8:29 say about the good that God wants to accomplish in your life?

6. Can you think of someone in the Bible who experienced God working things together for good in circumstances that were difficult or even evil? How does this encourage you?

7. If your security rests on something that can change, you can never rest securely. How is this true? As you look at the last week, have you practically been resting in Jesus and finding your joy and security in Him? Why or why not?

8. Read Psalm 16:11, Matthew 7:13-14, and John 14:6. How is the path of life also the path of joy?

9. You may want to make this verse your prayer as you continue on: "Show me your ways, O LORD, teach me your paths" (Ps. 25:4).

2

LOST AND FOUND: THE JOY OF SALVATION

On August 31, 1983, Korean Air Lines (KAL) flight 007 left the continental United States on a course for Seoul, Republic of Korea. After refueling in Anchorage, Alaska, the flight resumed.

Soon after departing from Anchorage, the aircraft began to deviate from its intended course. This slight deviation, spread over several hours in the air, resulted in the jet straying 185 miles off course. Apparently unaware of any impending danger, KAL 007 penetrated the airspace of the former Union of Soviet Socialist Republics (USSR).

Ground control in the USSR assumed the invading aircraft was a United States RC-135. As flight 007 approached Kamchatka peninsula, two Soviet fighters scrambled with orders to destroy the target. Two air-to-air missiles launched by one of the fighters struck the airplane, and it spiraled into the sea.

No evidence was found during the investigation to indicate the crew knew the flight was proceeding on the wrong course—although the flight's deviation continued for over five hours. According to the evidence, the crew inadvertently flew the entire flight on a constant magnetic heading controlled by autopilot.

The flight crew assumed their aircraft was following the right course, but their error resulted in the loss of many lives. Flight 007 never made its intended destination because it strayed away from the prescribed path.

A JET, SHEEP, AND PEOPLE

The Bible talks about a problem similar to that of flight 007. Instead of a jet that has strayed off course, it's people who have strayed off course. Using the analogy of sheep who have strayed away from their shepherd and become lost, the prophet, Isaiah, said, "We all, like sheep, have gone astray, each of us has turned to his own way" (53:6).

Whether it's a jet that deviates from its course or sheep that stray away from their shepherd, this is the picture: all of us have turned away from God to pursue our own paths.

Our continual pattern of straying away from God began when Adam sinned by disobeying God. "Therefore, just as sin entered the world through one man, and death through sin, and in this way death came to all men, because all sinned" (Rom. 5:12).

Adam's sin brought spiritual death to all of us and separated us from a holy God. "Your iniquities have separated you from your God" (Is. 59:2). To be separated from God is to be spiritually lost. When we are lost, we're unable to know the joy of belonging to the Shepherd. We can't walk the path of joy if we are not walking with Him.

Although the Bible tells us all people have strayed away from the Lord, many of us don't realize we're lost. Consequently, we feel no need to be rescued. Although we may not know we're lost, we still experience the symptoms of being separated from our Shepherd. We lack deep peace and sustaining joy. We feel anxious about life and search for meaning to our existence.

Since we don't like to experience (or acknowledge) these symptoms, we cover them up with busyness, work, family, recreation, possessions, and convince ourselves all is well. But this doesn't change the fact that we are still lost and unable to find our way home to God. The word *lost* describes the state of being separated from God, not a feeling.

I'LL DO IT MY WAY

A main characteristic of being spiritually lost is the desire to do things our way. As Isaiah said, we have all turned to our "*own* way." When we're lost, we don't think, *What does God want?* We think, *What do I want?* Just as a plant that is bent in a certain direction will grow that way, all of us are bent away from God and lean toward wanting our own way.

This self-centered bent is what the Bible calls *sin*. Out of our self-centered pride comes lying, cheating, stealing, immorality, and a host of other sinful attitudes and behaviors.

When we think of the word *sin*, some of us might associate it with the worst crimes we hear about on the evening news. Whether sin makes headline news or is quietly committed in the mind, sin in any form is an affront to God.

The Bible tells us that sinful thoughts and actions are the result of a sinful heart. "The heart is deceitful above all things and beyond cure. Who can understand it?" (Jer. 17:9). Sin can't be attributed to playing violent computer games, an unstable home, feelings of alienation, or society in general. While those things may heighten the problem, the root problem of sin lies within our hearts.

Sin is any thought, word, or action that deviates from God's absolute righteousness. When I compare myself to God, I know I fall short of His righteous perfection. But I also know I'm not alone. "*All have sinned* and fall short of the glory of God" (Rom. 3:23 emphasis added). This verse tells us we all miss the mark of God's perfect, holy nature. In a similar vein, we read:

> There is *no one* righteous, *not even one*; there is *no one* who understands, *no one* who seeks God. *All have turned away*, they have together become worthless; there is *no one* who does good, *not even one* (Rom. 3:10-12, emphasis added).

These verses tell us that none of us is inherently righteous. We don't seek God's righteousness because we lack the understanding to realize we are lost. This portion of Scripture stands in stark contrast to the popular belief that people are basically good. God, who knows our hearts, tells us people are basically corrupt. If we were all essentially good people, wouldn't children be born with a natural eagerness to obey and to think of others before themselves?

We see our basic sinful nature played out in the interaction between two toddlers. A little child grabs a toy out of the hands of another child. Then the child who had the toy taken away from him grabs it back and yells, "Mine!" Screaming and hitting ensue as the two children have a tug-of-war over the toy.

When our son, Aaron, was two years old, I recall an instance when his lack of compliance was more innovative than blatant. My mom, who was visiting us, said to him, "Why don't you pick up your toys while I count to twenty?"

Aaron replied, "Grawma, why you not pick up the toys and I count to twenty?"

Children are selfish and disobedient (or look for creative ways to get their own way!) because they, like all of us, come into this world with a sinful nature that says, "I want my way."

SEARCH AND RESCUE MISSION

This basic sinful bent doesn't mean we are incapable of ever doing anything nice. But all of our efforts at trying to live a good life and do good things won't change the fact that we are still on the wrong path—separated from God. Just as flight 007 was lost and on a course of destruction, this path will also lead to ruin. "Destruction and misery are in their paths, and the path of peace have they not known" (Rom. 3:16-17 NASB). The result of continuing on this path is eternal separation from the presence of God and His everlasting joy.

Because God loves us and desires us to glorify Him and enjoy Him, He came to rescue us from our lost condition. Since lost people can't find the Lord, He came to find us. Jesus left heaven and came to earth on a search and rescue mission on our behalf. Jesus explained His mission like this: "For the Son of Man came to seek and to save what was lost" (Luke 19:10).

Like everyone else, I was once spiritually lost. But now I am found. Jesus rescued me from my lost condition and brought me into a relationship of love with Him. He saved me from my path of destruction and placed me on His path of joy. This is how it happened.

LOST AND FOUND

When I was growing up, I went to church, read my Bible, and even memorized verses. I believed Jesus died on a cross and rose from the dead. But during my teenage years, I started to feel like I didn't need God. He didn't seem relevant to my life or interesting.

When I went away to college, I determined to do what I wanted to do—have a good time. Part of my good time included whether I would drink or smoke marijuana. I wanted to make the "right" decision, so I thought about it for a long time. During the months I pondered this, I knew the Lord was seeking me. Like a blinking red light the thought, *Read the Bible,* repeatedly flashed through my mind. This bothered me a lot. I didn't want to read the Bible.

In an effort to silence this persistent voice, I opened the Bible one day and said, "See God, there is nothing in here for me!" Then I slammed the Bible shut.

Still, He came after me.

Next, God began to cramp my fun. (Of course, I called sin "fun.") Every time I sinned, I felt guilty. I didn't like feeling this way, so I told God, "Leave me alone."

Still, He came after me.

One day as I was walking through the college lounge on my way to dinner, I heard a man say, "Jesus Christ." Immediately, I stopped and turned around. *Who said that?* I thought. I was used to hearing people say Jesus' name—it was usually surrounded with expletives. This time there was something different about the way His name was said. I didn't know what it was, but I felt compelled to find the man who had said Jesus Christ.

I quickly scanned the lounge for the man who had said Jesus' name, but I couldn't find him. My determination to find him quickly turned to desperation. I thought, *I have to find out who said Jesus Christ. I must find out!* The pull inside me was so strong, I could think of nothing else but to search for this man.

Then I spotted him. In the corner of the room, a man was talking to a handful of students who were seated around him. As I reached the group, he finished speaking. I walked up to him, and we began to talk. When he asked for my telephone number so someone could talk with me some more about Jesus, I gave it to him—even though I didn't care to hear any more.

Still, He came after me.

A few days later, a woman named Carol called me. She told me that the man I had previously met had given her my number. Over the next couple of months, Carol kept in contact with me through telephone calls and visits. When she asked me to accompany her on a weekend retreat, I agreed to go.

The first night at the retreat I was sure I'd made a huge mistake. The speaker seemed to drone on forever. I squirmed in my chair. Checked my watch. Yawned.

I thought I wasn't hearing what the speaker was saying, but I must have been listening. When he spoke about Jesus' death on the cross, I felt like something inside of me shattered. Suddenly the horrible realization of my sin crashed upon me. For the first time, I saw my unvarnished sin for what it was. I saw myself. All I could think was, *Oh no, what have I done? What have I done?*

Then, as though watching a parade go by, I began to think about specific sins I had committed. As I mentally viewed each sin, I was filled with tremendous remorse. I asked God to forgive me and told Him that I never wanted to do those things again.

Next, the Holy Spirit showed me that my sin had hurt Jesus. I knew Jesus had died on a cross for sin. But for the first time I understood the awful reality that *my* sin put Him on that cross as if I had pounded the nails through His hands myself. *I* was the sinner Jesus died for. The pain of knowing I had hurt Him deeply grieved me. I was broken with sorrow.

Although I had caused Jesus to suffer, I didn't experience His condemnation. Instead, I experienced a deep love that melted my heart. I couldn't resist Him any longer, and I didn't want to.

Right then, as the speaker wound up his talk, I bowed my head and silently prayed, "Lord, I don't ever want to hurt You again. From now on I just want to live for You and do what You want me to do." At that moment, the course of my life was forever changed. I entered the path of life and joy through faith in Jesus Christ.

I know Jesus came to seek and to save the lost, because when I was lost He sought me. And when He found me, He picked me up and rescued me. I am no longer lost, and I won't ever be lost again (John 10:29; Heb. 7:25).

How can I thank my Lord for coming after me and rescuing me from my lost condition? What words can express my gratitude over Jesus saving me? The words of the psalmist may say it best: "Then my soul will rejoice in the LORD and delight in his salvation. My whole being will exclaim, 'Who is like you, O LORD?' " (Ps. 35:9-10).

To discover how you can also be rescued and have all of your sins forgiven, I invite you to turn right now to "The Relationship You Were Created to Enjoy" on page 184.

HOW GOD DELIVERS US

Martyn Lloyd-Jones explains in his book, *The Life of Joy,* how God seeks us, awakens us to our lost condition, and delivers us from our sin.

> The first thing that God does is to awaken us to our state and condition. God the Holy Spirit acts on us and makes us see that we are guilty before God; we are lost. He makes us see that we are without life and that we do not know God. He makes us see that even our interest in God is something sinful, because we regard God as a term and do not hesitate to criticize him. The Holy Spirit awakens us to our need. There is a quickening that comes to us; we begin to see ourselves as we really are, and that in turn leads us to a state of repentance and sorrow for sin.

> Then the Holy Spirit creates within us a desire for God, a desire for a different order of life, a better life. We realize suddenly that we have been living a small self-centered life outside of God; we see the danger of it, the dread possibilities that will follow such a life, and we begin to long for a knowledge of God. We long to be delivered from this sin that we now see enchaining and fettering us. We try to find God but we discover we cannot. And then the Holy Spirit does the blessed work of revealing Christ to us in all the perfection of his work. He suddenly opens our eyes to see the real meaning of Christ and his cross; he shows the objective work that was done there once and forever, and he applies that all to us. He makes us realize that this is not something theoretical, but something that is of momentous concern to us.
>
> And then he does something which is, in a sense, still more wonderful. He forgives us our sins. He brings into being a new life within us; we are aware of a new man, a new nature.[1]

First, God reveals to us our sinfulness and the utter hopelessness of our lost condition. Then the Holy Spirit enables us to turn from our sin to Jesus, and God gives us the gift of faith to trust in Jesus Christ as our Lord and Savior. At that moment, we are no longer lost. We are found. Rescued. Saved. "For he has rescued us from the dominion of darkness and brought us into the kingdom of the Son he loves, in whom we have redemption, the forgiveness of sins" (Col. 1:13-14).

Sometimes people refer to becoming a Christian as "finding the Lord." But the Lord was never lost—we were! From the time God first sought Adam (Gen. 3:9), He has always taken the initiative to seek lost sinners. God was pursuing you and me before we ever gave Him a second thought. Throughout both the Old and New Testament, we see God is by nature a seeking Savior. In Ezekiel 34, we read:

> I myself will search for my sheep and look after them...I will rescue them from all the places where they were scattered on a day of clouds and darkness...I will search for the lost and bring back the strays (vs. 11,12,16).

GOD'S SEEKING HEART

In Luke 15, Jesus told three parables that illustrate God's heart to seek and to save the lost. As we focus on two of these parables, we will see God's joy in saving the sinner and our joy over receiving His salvation.

Jesus said,

> "Suppose one of you has a hundred sheep and loses one of them. Does he not leave the ninety-nine in the open country and go after the lost sheep until he finds it? And when he finds it, he joyfully puts it on his shoulders and goes home. Then he calls his friends and neighbors together and says, 'Rejoice with me; I have found my lost sheep.' I tell you that in the same way there will be more rejoicing in heaven over one sinner who repents than over ninety-nine righteous persons who do not need to repent" (vs. 4-7).

In this parable, we see God's compassionate heart, as represented by the shepherd, to seek the lost. The shepherd didn't shrug his shoulders over the one lost sheep. He was greatly concerned over his lost sheep. In the same way, one lost person matters greatly to God.

As I write about sheep, I can't help but think of a sheep

named Curly that my family had when I was little. Because our house was set among woods and hills, many places couldn't be reached with a lawnmower. Curly ate the grass in the areas where a lawnmower couldn't go.

When I came home from school in the afternoon, I would often look for Curly so I could play with him. Sometimes I wouldn't see him right away, so I'd climb over the fence, walk down the hill, and look for him. When I found Curly, I'd give his big, wooly body a hug. My memories of Curly help me to realize how a shepherd would become attached to his sheep. It also helps me to see God's deep concern over one lost person.

In the parable of the lost sheep, we don't see the sheep making any effort to seek the shepherd. I know Curly never looked for me. A lost sheep has no ability to seek the shepherd. The shepherd must seek the sheep or it will never be found. Likewise, Jesus came to seek us because we had no ability to find Him.

The shepherd, in Luke 15, put his deep concern for one stray sheep into action. He left the rest of his flock to search for his lost sheep. We can picture the shepherd straining his eyes as he searches the horizon for his sheep. He looks in caves and peers into ravines. Then he spies his sheep, caught in a thorn bush. The shepherd smiles as he gently untangles his sheep. He strokes his sheep and talks tenderly to it. Then he joyfully lifts the exhausted sheep onto his shoulders and carries it home.

As the shepherd approaches the village, he calls out to his friends and neighbors, "Rejoice with me; I have found my lost sheep" (Luke 15:6). The shepherd is so filled with joy over rescuing his lost sheep that his joy spills over onto all those around him.

The shepherd doesn't silently creep into town for a solitary celebration. Did you ever try to keep good news to yourself? It's nearly impossible, isn't it? The shepherd jubilantly parades his lost sheep before his friends and neighbors, and together they enjoy his victory celebration.

In the second parable, in Luke 15, Jesus told a similar story about a woman who searched for a lost coin. He said,

> "Or suppose a woman has ten silver coins and loses one. Does she not light a lamp, sweep the house and search carefully until she finds it? And when she finds it, she calls her friends and neighbors together and says, 'Rejoice with me; I have found my lost coin.' In the same way, I tell you, there is rejoicing in the presence of the angels of God over one sinner who repents" (vs. 8-10).

Like the shepherd, we can picture the woman diligently searching for her lost coin. She sweeps under her furniture. She looks on all of her shelves and scours every corner. When it becomes dark, she lights a lamp and continues her pursuit into the night. Then she spots the coin, wedged between the folds of her rug.

The woman leans down, grabs the coin, and runs excitedly from her home. Like the shepherd, she invites her friends and neighbors to come and celebrate with her. She holds her coin up in the air and shouts, "Rejoice with me; I have found my lost coin" (Luke 15:9). The woman's joy over finding her lost coin fills the village.

GOD'S JOY OVER RESCUING A LOST PERSON

If the shepherd and the woman were filled with joy over finding a sheep and a coin, think about the joy God has over seeking and saving a lost person! When God finds us—all tangled up and exhausted—He gently takes us into His arms, lifts us onto His shoulders, and carries us home.

Then a great victory celebration breaks forth in heaven. God invites the angels, represented as friends and neighbors, to share in His joy. One lost person who is found causes heaven to rejoice. "In the same way, I tell you, there is rejoicing in the presence of the angels of God over one sinner who repents" (Luke 15:10).

As we look at these two parables, who experienced the greater joy—the friends and neighbors or the shepherd and the woman? The shepherd and the woman experienced the greater joy because they actually sought and found what was lost. Their joy was the highest because they had made the highest investment. The friends and neighbors shared in the overflowing joy of the shepherd and the woman.

God the Father invested everything He had—the life of His Son—to seek and to save us. Can we imagine God's tremendous joy over saving a person for whom Christ died? Every time God saves one who was lost, His unbridled joy spills throughout heaven. The angels gather before God's throne to celebrate in the overflow of His joy.

These parables show us that God is a God of great joy. Some of us, however, may not view God as One who continually experiences boundless joy. We think God expresses about as much joy as a stone face on Mount Rushmore. These parables indicate that the opposite is true. God isn't made of granite. He is the God of joy who desires us to know His joy. Is this your view of God?

As the shepherd and the woman experienced great joy, so does God. But God doesn't merely experience joy. He is the source of joy. All joy in the universe emanates from God, who is exceedingly glad!

The angels in heaven don't rejoice while God sits by and observes. *He* initiates the celebration. When the angels look at the face of the Lord when a sinner repents, they see His joyous expression of immense pleasure. God continually rejoices in His triumph over rescuing lost sinners, and the angels share in His joy. Heaven is a place of endless, unlimited joy!

God initially rejoiced when He saved us. And we can be confident His joy over saving us doesn't diminish with time. God's joy doesn't start out strong and then fade as the years go by. Listen to what this verse says about His joy: "The LORD your God is with you, he is mighty to save. He will take great delight in you, he will quiet you with his love, he will rejoice over you with singing" (Zeph. 3:17). God's continual joy over saving you and me is the expression of His continual love for us.

OUR RESPONSE TO BEING RESCUED

The two parables we've looked at from Luke 15 show us that God and the angels in heaven rejoice when one sinner repents. But what about us down here on earth? What is our response to God saving us?

Join The Celebration: Rejoice

If the angels rejoice as the *observers* of salvation, think how much greater our rejoicing should be as the recipients who *experience* salvation. Angels are "ministering spirits sent to serve those who will inherit salvation" (Heb. 1:14). We who have been saved by Jesus are those heirs (Rom. 8:17). Angels don't receive God's grace, mercy, and forgiveness. We have received these from God and more. As His own sons and daughters, we are able to know the joy of an intimate relationship with God, who we call "Father" (Rom. 8:15).

As we rejoice in the Lord of our salvation, we walk in step with His joy. "Let us rejoice and be glad in his salvation" (Is. 25:9). God wants our lives down here synchronized with what is happening up there. As our lives exhibit joy, we live consistently with the celebration taking place before the throne of God.

Each time the Chicago Bulls won a National Basketball Association championship, a huge celebration was held along Chicago's lakefront. While the celebrations were taking place, it was impossible to drive anywhere near the vicinity and not notice hundreds of thousands of people packed into Grant Park and the surrounding area.

Sadly, some of us go through life and give little thought to the celebration in heaven. We bypass the festivities and don't join in. In Psalm 13, David joined in the celebration by saying, "But I trust in your unfailing love; *my heart rejoices in your salvation.* I will sing to the LORD, for he has been good to me" (vs. 5-6 emphasis added). Do you rejoice in your salvation? Do you praise the Lord for His goodness in rescuing you from your lost condition?

Heaven is a place of rejoicing and celebration. But God doesn't want us to wait until we're in heaven before we start to celebrate. As we "rejoice in the Lord" (Phil. 4:4), we walk in step with the rhythm of heaven. When we rejoice in the Lord of our salvation, we glorify the One who saved us because He is displayed as the source of our joy.

Salvation is a source of endless joy for the believer. The psalmist declared, "My heart rejoices in your salvation" (13:5). If God never gave us anything else (yet He has), to have eternal life in Jesus Christ is reason enough for us to rejoice forever. Jesus said "Rejoice that your names are written in heaven" (Luke 10:20).

Remember What The Lord Has Done: Thank Him

Do you remember the joy and thankfulness that filled your heart when the Lord first saved you? My husband can still recall the heartfelt thanks of a lost girl he found in a forest preserve. Dean teaches high school and coaches girls' cross-country. One afternoon after the girls had completed running through a forest preserve, he noticed Kelly was missing. Immediately, Dean ran into the forest looking for Kelly and shouting her name.

When Dean found Kelly, she was wandering along with no idea where she was going. When Kelly saw Dean, she was overjoyed. "Oh, Coach, am I ever glad to see you! Thank you for coming after me and finding me!"

We want to remember that the Lord came after us at the expense of His own life. An attitude of thanksgiving for remembering His sacrifice for us keeps our relationship with Him fresh and vibrant. Thanking Him for saving us is a safeguard that prevents us from taking our salvation for granted. If we don't continually thank Him, we will become cool in our love for Him and fall into the trap that ensnared the Ephesian church.

In the second chapter of Revelation, Jesus gave this message through the Apostle John to the church at Ephesus: "Yet I hold this against you: You have forsaken your first love" (v. 4). Although the Ephesians maintained high morals and sound doctrine, they lacked a deep love for the Lord. The Ephesians forgot the joy they experienced when they first came to know Christ. They neglected to thank the Lord and praise Him for rescuing them. Consequently, their passion for Jesus began to fade. When their love for Him cooled, they no longer experienced the joy of an intimate relationship with Him.

Jesus' rebuke to the church at Ephesus sharply contrasts with Paul's letter to the Ephesians thirty-five years earlier. In the first chapter of that book, Paul said he continually thanked God for their faith and love for one another (vs. 15-16). But in the span of a few decades, the Ephesians had jumbled their priorities and forgotten what was most important: a deep love for Jesus. How this must have grieved the heart of the Lord.

J. Oswald Sanders noted:

> The danger of falling out of love with Christ is no less present in our times, and it occasions our Lord as much grief now as then. Intimacy with God is a fragile thing that must be carefully guarded.[2]

As we thank the Lord for saving us, our hearts remain tender toward Him, and we foster the joy of an intimate relationship with Him. The Shepherd who sought and saved us still carries us in His arms and desires us to enjoy intimacy with Him. "He tends his flock like a shepherd: He gathers the lambs in his arms and carries them close to his heart" (Is. 40:11).

You and I celebrate because Jesus has rescued us. We give thanks because He has opened our blind eyes. We rejoice because we are no longer lost, but found.

The well-known song, *Amazing Grace*, by John Newton eloquently describes our lost condition and reminds us of the joy of being found:

> Amazing grace! How sweet the sound
> That saved a wretch like me!
> I once was lost, but now am found,
> Was blind, but now I see.[3]

Out of gratefulness for his salvation, the psalmist declared, "Come, let us sing for joy to the LORD; let us shout aloud to the Rock of our salvation. Let us come before him with thanksgiving and extol him with music and song" (95:1-2).

Following in the footsteps of this Psalm, the final verse of *Amazing Grace* says,

When we've been there ten thousand years,
Bright shining as the sun,
We've no less days to sing God's praise
Than when we first begun.

Let's celebrate and sing for joy to the Lord!

Responding to God's Word

1. What do lost people have in common with KAL flight 007? What characterizes lost people?

2. Many people believe they are basically good, but sometimes make mistakes. What does God say about this in Romans 3:10-12? Why do you think this is so hard for people to accept?

3. Read "The Relationship You Were Created to Enjoy" on page 184. How would you explain the way of salvation to a friend?

4. What did you learn about God's seeking heart from the parables in Luke 15 that encouraged you?

5. Some people don't view God as One who is exceedingly glad and continually rejoicing. What did you think God was like before you became a Christian? How do you think learning about God's immense joy will impact your relationship with Him?

6. Read Colossians 3:1-2. How do you think you can become more focused on the joy of heaven? How will this affect the way you live today?

7. What happens to your relationship with the Lord if you take your salvation for granted? On a scale of 1-10, with one being the lowest and ten being the highest, rate your joy over the Lord saving you.

8. The following suggestions may help you to experience greater joy in the Lord of your salvation:

    - Read Psalm 13:5-6. Ask God to fill you with joy and appreciation.

    - Find the words *joy* and *rejoicing* in a Bible concordance. Look up the corresponding verses to see what the Bible says, specifically in regard to salvation.

- Read the account of Jesus' crucifixion in Matthew 27, Mark 15, Luke 23, and John 19. Write down your thoughts.

- Remember what you were like before God saved you. Ephesians 2:1-3.

- Thank Him each day for saving you. Psalm 9:1-2.

- Think about God's joy over saving you, and live in step with His joy.

3

THE JOY OF KNOWING GOD

Andre-Francois Raffray, 47, a lawyer from Arles, France, thought he had made the deal of a lifetime. In 1965 he signed a contract with Jeanne Calment, then 90, giving her $500 a month for life on the condition that she leave him her house when she died. Raffray died at 77, shortly after Calment became the world's oldest known living person. "We all make bad deals in life," Raffray said when Calment turned 120. He paid her over $180,000 in the deal; the house was worth about $60,000. Jeanne Calment died in 1997 at the age of 122.[1]

Many people spend their lives much like Raffray spent his money. They invest themselves in things that will ultimately bring disappointment. What can you and I invest ourselves in with the confidence of knowing it will produce joy? What pursuit is worthy of our affection and appreciation?

In the last chapter, we saw that Jesus took the initiative to seek and to save us. When we consider that Jesus left the glory of heaven to come and die for us, seeking us is obviously a high priority for Him.

Seeking to better know and love the Lord who first sought us is the highest privilege and joy of those He has saved. The psalmist said, "But may all who seek you rejoice and be glad in you; may those who love your salvation always say, 'The LORD be exalted!'" (40:16).

When the writers of the Bible spoke about seeking God, they were referring to a deep desire to know Him. To seek God is to express a longing for intimacy with Him. A seeking heart delights in God as the object of its affection. "Let the hearts of those who seek the LORD rejoice. Look to the LORD and his strength; seek his face always" (Ps. 105:3-4).

A longing to know God leads us deeper into our Father's heart of joy where we reap the rich benefit of enjoying an intimate relationship with Him. John MacArthur said, "You can set your heart ablaze with no loftier, more worthy ambition than the pursuit of an increasingly intimate knowledge of the God who created you."[2]

In this chapter, we are going to look at the Israelites at two different points in their history and see how they forfeited joy because they didn't know God according to the truth of His Word. We will learn how wrong thinking patterns about God also prevent us from enjoying intimacy with Him. We'll see how to remove these obstacles from our path so we can experience the joy of knowing God.

PERSONAL KNOWLEDGE OR DISTANT INFORMATION

Let's start by looking at the difference between knowing information about God and personally knowing God. To help illustrate this difference, let's think about our knowledge of Abraham Lincoln. If we have grown up in the United States, we have learned information about Lincoln. When my family and I visited a museum that featured memorabilia from Lincoln's life, I gained additional knowledge about him.

At the museum, I read some of Lincoln's original writings and learned interesting facts about him and his family. I was especially fascinated to see the chair Lincoln sat in the night he was shot. I stared at the chair for so long, I didn't realize my family had moved to another room in the museum!

Although I enjoyed learning facts about Lincoln's life, when I left the museum I was no different from when I had entered it. The information I learned about Lincoln didn't change my life or affect how I make decisions.

Many people know about God in the same way they know about Lincoln. They know information about God, but they don't personally know *Him*. Although they believe certain facts about God, those facts don't influence how they live or make decisions. They have a knowledge of God, but lack an experiential, life-changing knowledge of Him that transforms their whole being and produces joy.

FACTS WITHOUT FEELINGS

In the first chapter of Isaiah, we discover that the Israelites had an intellectual knowledge of God—much like my knowledge of Lincoln—but what they knew about God didn't affect their hearts. The Israelites carried out their religious ceremonies, yet their hearts were emotionally distant from God. As a result, God pronounced this indictment against them: "The ox knows his master, the donkey his owner's manger, but Israel does not know, my people do not understand" (v. 3).

God rebuked the Israelites for not knowing Him at the most basic level—as a donkey knows its master. Their emotional apathy toward the Lord showed they didn't know or understand the first thing about Him. If the Israelites had known God, they would have understood and obeyed His command to "Love the LORD your God with *all your heart* and with all your soul and with all your strength" (Deut. 6:5 emphasis added).

The Israelites met the external requirements of the law, but they disobeyed God's basic internal requirement to love Him with all their hearts. Because the Israelites disobeyed God on this basic point, they weren't able to know the joy of a close relationship with Him. Joy is the overflow of a heart that loves the Lord and longs to know Him more intimately.

The Israelites were adept at going through the motions of worshiping God, but they lacked affection for the God they thought they were worshiping. Because the Israelites lacked a heartfelt love for God, He rejected their meaningless worship. God told them, "The multitude of your sacrifices—what are they to me?...Stop bringing meaningless offerings!" (Is. 1:11,13).

The Israelites thought well of themselves for being so religious. They assumed God was as pleased with them as they were with themselves. In truth, the Lord despised their mechanics. "Your New Moon festivals and your appointed feasts my soul hates. They have become a burden to me; I am weary of bearing them" (Is. 1:14).

They offered God their rituals, but they didn't offer Him their hearts. God didn't want their sacrifices. He wanted hearts that loved Him and longed to know Him. "For I delight in loyalty rather than sacrifice, and in the knowledge of God rather than burnt offerings" (Hosea 6:6 NASB).

Martyn Lloyd Jones said,

> What God wants is our hearts. He does not want our burnt offerings and sacrifices as such; He does not want our theoretical and intellectual interest in Himself; He does not want us just to be arguing theology. No, no! He wants our hearts![3]

The Israelites performed their religious ceremonies, but they felt no emotion for the Lord. I can hardly imagine how awful I would feel if Dean went through the motions of being a husband, but his heart was emotionally cold. I would feel so sad if my husband spoke to me because he felt obligated. How hurt I would feel if he saw living with me as a function to perform, instead of a relationship to enjoy.

Think about how the Lord feels if we view Him as an obligation, instead of a Person to know and enjoy. As love is basic to an enjoyable marriage, so a heartfelt love for the Lord is basic to enjoying intimacy with Him. Dr. Lloyd-Jones said, "Christianity is not obeying a set of moral duties—it is a passionate relationship with the most appealing Person in the universe, Jesus Christ."[4]

God wanted the Israelites to know *Him*—not just information about Him. God desired them to worship Him within the context of a loving relationship. Within that framework, the Lord desired them to grow in their love for Him and to experience the joy of a satisfying relationship with Him. The Israelites didn't love the Lord from their hearts, so they missed the joy of knowing Him.

AN INTIMATE KNOWLEDGE OF GOD

What does it mean to know God? Jesus, in the final hours before the cross, said to the Father, "Now this is eternal life: that they may *know you*, the only true God, and Jesus Christ, whom you have sent" (John 17:3 emphasis added)

In this verse, Jesus spoke about eternal life as knowing God. Eternal life isn't *something* we receive, but *Someone* we receive—Jesus Christ, who makes us spiritually alive. When we receive eternal life, we enter into a relationship of knowing and enjoying the living God. When Jesus referred to knowing God, He was talking about personal, experiential knowledge of Him.

This personal knowledge of God is similar to Adam's knowledge of his wife, Eve. In Genesis, we read: "Now Adam knew Eve his wife, and she conceived and bore Cain" (4:1 NKJV). This verse doesn't mean Adam knew some information about Eve. When Adam knew Eve, she became pregnant. The word *knew* refers to the intimate relationship between a husband and wife that results in conception.

Similarly, when we know God, we have a spiritual oneness with Him that results in our ability to enjoy an intimate relationship of love with Him. The Apostle Paul wrote: "But the man who loves God is known by God" (1 Cor. 8:3). This verse describes the most intimate of all relationships—our union with the Lord. We know Him within the context of a personal, loving relationship.

In Galatians, we read: "But now that you know God—or rather are known by God" (4:9). To know God, and to be known by God describes the mutuality of the intimate love relationship we share with Him.

J. Oswald Sanders said,

> Mutual love is the essence of intimacy. Where there is no love, there is no intimacy...In its essence, love is "the self-imparting quality in the nature of God that moves Him to seek the highest good of His creatures, in whom He seeks to awaken responsive love." Because of that, love is basic to our knowledge of and intimacy with God.

> "The one who does not love does not know God, for God is love" (1 John 4:8). Love is grounded in the nature of God and is the highest expression of character. We are mature only to the degree that we are mature in love.[5]

Think of the heartfelt love of a young man that compels him to pursue knowing the young lady he cares about. Yet the woman who is so fair and lovely will, at some time, be unkind, thoughtless, and selfish.

How much more we should pursue knowing the Lord who selflessly gave His life for us. Although we are thoughtless toward Him, His love for us remains constant. He will always be good and kind. Let's ask the Lord to give us a passion to pursue knowing Him so we will know the joy of walking closely with our Beloved.

A LONGING FOR GOD'S WORD

The primary way we grow in our knowledge of God is through the Bible. Many verses in Psalm 119 show us the deep longing of the psalmist to know God. This Psalm also reveals to us the joy the psalmist received through God's Word:

> Blessed [joyful] are they who keep his statutes and seek him with all their heart (v. 2).
>
> My soul is consumed with longing for your laws at all times (v. 20).
>
> For I delight in your commands because I love them (v. 47).
>
> I open my mouth and pant, longing for your commands (v. 131).
>
> I rejoice in your promise like one who finds great spoil (v. 162).

The writer of Psalm 119 saw God's Word as a source of great joy and refreshment. The psalmist's joy in God's Word sprang out of the longing of his heart to know the Lord.

Like the psalmist, we want to view our time in God's Word as the opportunity to experience the joy of knowing God better and loving Him more. Otherwise, like the Israelites, our time in His Word can become mechanical. We may start to view our relationship with Jesus as something to maintain, rather than Someone to enjoy.

This was the case with Mindy (name changed). I hardly knew Mindy when she called and asked me if I would meet her at a restaurant. After we ordered our food, Mindy told me she had attended a Christian high school and had memorized the entire book of Proverbs.

Then, in a matter-of-fact way, she mentioned that in recent years she had been reading her Bible less and not at all for the previous couple of months. Mindy said she was seeing behaviors and attitudes in her life that she didn't like. She was frustrated and discontent and wanted to know if I could help her. As Mindy and I finished our sandwiches, we set up a time for me to come to her house.

As I drove home from the restaurant, I asked God to give me wisdom on what to tell Mindy. If I told her to read her Bible, I thought she would probably do it. But her relationship with the Lord would still not be right. The issue wasn't to get her to read her Bible. The primary issue was that her heart wasn't right.

Years earlier, Mindy had diligently read her Bible and even memorized large portions of Scripture. But she had pursued knowing the Lord as an academic assignment. Mindy lacked a heartfelt passion for the Lord she was memorizing verses about. Consequently, Mindy's relationship with the Lord had become stiff and mechanical, and the joy had drained out of her life like water out of a bathtub.

I prayed all week about what to say to Mindy. I prayed as I drove to her house. As I knocked on Mindy's door, I took a deep breath and prayed once more. What I planned on saying to her wasn't going to be easy for either of us.

After Mindy found an activity to occupy her daughter, we made ourselves comfortable at her kitchen table. We began by talking about what it means to be a Christian.

Then I said, "Let's say that every night when Jim (name changed) comes home from work, you ignore him. Jim longs to hear about your day, and he wants to share his day with you. But you don't talk to him or listen to him. Because he loves you so passionately, he doesn't give up trying to get your attention. He leaves love notes around the house, but you don't read them. He calls you from work, but you don't answer the telephone. He desperately tries to communicate how much he loves you and desires to enjoy an intimate relationship with you, but you are indifferent. How do you think Jim feels?"

Mindy's eyes filled with tears. "If I treated Jim like that, I think he would feel terrible."

"Jesus loves you," I said, "and He desires to have an intimate relationship with you, but you are ignoring Him. He wants you to share every detail of your life with Him, but you don't take the time. He wants to tell you His thoughts, but you don't want to listen. He gives you His unceasing love every day, but you are too preoccupied to notice. How do you think Jesus feels?"

Tears rolled down Mindy's face. "I'm so sorry. I've hurt Jesus, haven't I?"

I urged Mindy to get alone with the Lord and confess her sin of grieving Him. Then before I left, I asked Mindy to call me during the week.

Later that week when I heard from Mindy, the inflection in her voice immediately told me things were different. "I've had the best week! I confessed my sin to God, and I've been reading my Bible every day. It's been wonderful. For the first time in so long, I'm experiencing real joy!"

I smiled and thanked God for what He did in Mindy's heart. Mindy's desire to know God through His Word sprang from a heart that now longed for Him.

OUR FATHER'S JOY

We generally look at our time in God's Word from our perspective and what we receive. Let's think for a moment of what spending focused time with God may look like from His perspective and what He receives.

Think about how a father feels when his little girl runs to greet him when he comes home from work. The little girl runs to her father because she loves him and is glad to see him. The father hugs his daughter and holds her close because he loves her, and he is glad she wants to be near him.

How much joy it brings to our Father's heart when we look at spending time with Him like a little girl running to greet her dad. If your time in God's Word isn't what you would like it to be, try this perspective: Sit down, open your Bible, and say, "Father, I'm reading my Bible today because I love you, and I desire to know You more intimately. Reveal Yourself to me so I will think your thoughts and feel what You feel. May we delight in the love we have for one another."

Do you and I delight in knowing God? Is He the joy of our hearts? Does the love of Christ compel us to seek intimacy with Him? Let's approach our time in God's Word as the prophet, Jeremiah, who said, "When your words came, I ate them; they were my joy and my heart's delight" (Jer. 15:16).

FEELINGS WITHOUT FACTS

We can't enjoy intimacy with the Lord unless our intellectual knowledge of Him touches our hearts. Joy is not found in emotionless, intellectual assent to information about God. On the other hand, joy is also not found in relying on our emotions apart from the facts of who God is.

We're going to look again at the Israelites at a different point in their history. This time we will see they were filled with emotion, but they still didn't know God and experience true joy because their feelings weren't aligned with truth. We want to avoid their pitfall and rely on God's Word to guide us into truth instead of our emotions.

In Exodus 32, the Israelites had grown tired of waiting for Moses to come down from Mount Sinai. They demanded Aaron to give them a god they could worship. In response to their demand, Aaron instructed the people to bring him their gold jewelry. Then he cast the gold into the shape of a calf. The next day, the people offered sacrifices to their calf god and indulged themselves in eating, drinking, and revelry (vs. 1-5).

When Moses came down from the mountain and saw the people running wild, he shouted, "Whoever is for the Lord, come to me" (Exodus 32:26). All the Levites came to Moses. Then the Levites went throughout the camp and killed three thousand of the people (v. 28).

The Israelites demonstrated plenty of emotion as they danced and sang before their calf god. But God was far from pleased with their display. Their emotional fanfare angered God because their feelings were not aligned with truth.

While Moses was receiving the Ten Commandments, the Israelites were disobeying the first three commandments by putting another god before the Lord, making an idol, and worshiping it

(Exodus 20:3-5). Although they were dancing merrily, they were not experiencing true joy because the God of joy was displeased with them.

Instead of conforming their lives to God's Word and worshiping Him in truth, they chose to worship a flexible god they could mold into any shape. The Israelites didn't stop to think about who the true God is and what He desires. They preferred instead to sculpt a god according to their own desires.

The Israelites trusted in their feelings to guide them, rather than the facts of God's Word. This resulted in emotion-based religion without knowledge of the true God. "My people are destroyed from lack of knowledge" (Hosea 4:6). Again, the Israelites forfeited a relationship of joy with the Lord because they didn't know Him according to the truth of who He is.

CLAY GODS

Just as the Israelites fashioned a god according to their feelings, many people today fashion their view of God according to how they feel. This relative view of truth is prevalent in our society and rapidly gaining momentum.

The unexpected conversation I had one morning with the owner of an antiques store exemplifies the popularity of trusting in feelings over truth. As I picked up a dish and turned it over to check the price, the woman who owned the store said to me, "Maybe the reason I like antiques so much is because I lived in another time. Who knows? I might have been on the Titanic."

She may have expected me to nod my head and reply, "Maybe I was on the Titanic with you." But before I had a chance to say anything, her telephone rang. I wanted to respond to what she said, but she kept on talking. I prayed, "Lord, please make her hang up, and show me what to say." After I finished looking at everything in the store, she was still talking. I finally picked up a $2 handkerchief and walked to the counter.

When she hung up the telephone to make the sale, we chatted for a few minutes about antiques. Then I asked her about the basis of her belief. She told me her belief was based on what she felt. When I wondered aloud whether she had always found her feelings to be reliable, she acknowledged her feelings weren't always accurate.

As we talked some more, she told me she felt she believed in God and felt she was going to heaven. Before I left, I briefly told her how Jesus had changed my life and gave her a written explanation of the gospel that I had with me.

This woman's mystical, feeling-based approach to truth is readily accepted in our society. We often hear people say one person's truth may not be true for another. Instead of lining up their lives with the absolute truth of God's Word, truth is seen as something flexible. Truth, like clay, is bent, twisted, stretched, and molded into any shape to fit a person's mood, circumstance, or lifestyle.

Consequently, many people shape their "truth" about God according to how they feel. They may feel they know God and may, at times, feel they are close to Him. But if they don't believe the truth of who God is, as revealed in the Bible, they don't know God. What they know are the ideas they have molded about God—not God Himself. These false ideas prevent people from knowing God and the joy He gives to those who believe in Him as He is.

When people separate God from the truth of His Word and invent their own ideas about Him, they worship a clay figurine or a golden calf. No matter how sincere their feelings may be—to believe unbiblical ideas about God is idolatry.

A.W. Tozer gives us this insight from his book, *The Knowledge of the Holy*:

> Let us beware lest we in our pride accept the erroneous notion that idolatry consists only in kneeling before visible objects of adoration, and that civilized peoples are therefore free from it. The essence of idolatry is the entertainment of thoughts about God that are unworthy of Him.[6]

Untrue or unworthy ideas about God prevent people from knowing God as He is and enjoying a true relationship with Him. To know God in truth, we embrace both the facts about Him, as revealed in the Bible, and an experiential relationship of love with Him through Jesus Christ.

LOVING GOD WITH OUR MINDS

In the Bible, we see the importance of knowing and loving God with our whole being, which includes our minds as well as our heart and soul. Jesus said, "You shall love the Lord your God with all your heart and with all your soul and with *all your mind*" (Matt. 22:37 emphasis added). J. Oswald Sanders noted: "The flame of our love for God and our fellow men must be fed by fuel provided by the mind. Our love and worship of God must not be merely intuitive. We must put intelligence into it."[7]

God's Word is the fuel we put into our minds that causes our hearts to burn with love for Him. We feed our love for the Lord by filling our minds with truth and by applying His truth to our lives. A Christian is someone who:

- Has "come to a knowledge of the truth" (1 Tim. 2:4).
- Loves the truth. "For I delight in your commands because I love them" (Ps. 119:47).

- Pursues the truth. "But grow in the grace and knowledge of our Lord and Savior Jesus Christ" (2 Peter 3:18).

As believers, we want to line up our feelings with the truth. As we fill our minds with God's truth, He fills our hearts with His joy. Charles Spurgeon commented in his book, *The Fullness of Joy*, on the connection between knowing and studying God's truth and our experience of comfort and joy:

> The knowledge of the love of God, the knowledge of the full Atonement made on Calvary, the knowledge of the eternal covenant, the knowledge of the immutable faithfulness of Jehovah—indeed, all knowledge that reveals God in His relationship to His people—will tend to create comfort in the hearts of His saints. Therefore, do not be careless about scriptural doctrine. Study the Word, and seek to understand the mind of the Spirit as revealed in it, for this blessed Book was written for your learning, that "*through patience and comfort of the scriptures* [you] *might have hope*" (Romans 15:4). If you are diligent students of the Word, you will find that you have good reason to rejoice in the Lord in all circumstances (author's emphasis).[8]

THE PATH OF TRUE JOY

In contrast to what Spurgeon said about the joy and comfort we receive from filling our minds with the knowledge of God's Word, the prevalent mindset of the day is the motto: "If it feels good, do it." We live in an age where feelings and experiences are seen as legitimate indicators of truth.

This attitude has invaded the church and affected our thinking. If we feel like obeying the Lord, we do. If not, we don't. If we feel like reading our Bible, we do. If we don't feel like it, we wait until we do.

For instance, a friend of mine told me about a woman she knows who commented, "I feel closest to the Lord when I'm driving in my car."

My friend asked her, "What about when you read your Bible?"

The woman responded, "If I don't feel like reading my Bible, I just think about the Lord when I'm in the car."

Of course, it's good to think about the Lord when we drive, or in whatever we do. But we need to fill our minds with His Word so our thoughts dwell on what is true. We need to align our thoughts with the Bible, so we contemplate truth instead of dreamy feelings. Let's face it, it's much easier to dream about God than to read and study the Bible. But dreaming about God is not the path of joy or the way to know Him.

Joy is not a mystical feeling. Joy is based on knowing and believing concrete facts about who God is. Joy is the response that the Holy Spirit produces in us, as we focus our minds on God's truth and apply it to our lives. "The precepts of the LORD are right, giving joy to the heart" (Ps. 19:8).

God's Word is the path of true joy. "Direct me in the path of your commands, for there I find delight" (Ps. 119:35).

THE RIGHT THING

If we pursue knowing God only when we feel like it, we compartmentalize our relationship with Him into a mystical realm that is disconnected from real life. For example, if your baby daughter cried in the middle of the night, would you sit on the edge of your bed and decide whether to feed your baby based on how you felt? Of course not. You would get up and feed your baby.

When our daughter, Whitney, was born, she was nursing every half hour and taking just two twenty minute naps a day. With her frequent feedings, infrequent naps, and also caring for our son, Aaron, I was past the point of exhaustion! But when I heard Whitney cry for the fourth time in the middle of the night, I climbed out of bed and fed her because I loved her and feeding her was the right thing to do.

In a similar way, we spend focused time with the Lord because we love Him and feeding ourselves from His Word is the right thing to do. We pick up our Bible and read it because this is how we grow and get to know the Lord we love. Just as a baby grows from drinking milk, we also grow from drinking in the milk of God's Word. "Like newborn babes, crave pure spiritual milk, so that by it you may grow in your salvation" (1 Peter 2:2).

Because we love the Lord, we make a decision to spend time with Him and to know Him better. When we love someone, we do things for the sake of the relationship—whether it's feeding our baby or feeding ourselves from God's Word.

A heartfelt love for the Lord motivates us to pursue knowing Him through His Word. We, therefore, discipline ourselves to pick up our Bible and read it so we can better know the Lord we love. Love motivates us to take action, and discipline carries it out. Our love for God and our knowledge of Him is both emotional and volitional. "I delight in your decrees; I will not neglect your word" (Ps. 119:16).

Let's look at our own lives. Are we ruled by our emotions or the Lord? What is more reliable, our feelings or God's Word? Feelings are subjective and prone to change. God's Word is objective and never changes. We know God and enjoy our relationship with Him through the truth of His Word.

A LIFE OF JOY

In Psalm 1, the psalmist shows us the joy of knowing God by drinking in His Word:

> Blessed [joyful] is the man who does not walk in the counsel of the wicked or stand in the way of sinners or

> sit in the seat of mockers. But his delight is in the law of the LORD, and on his law he meditates day and night. He is like a tree planted by streams of water, which yields its fruit in season and whose leaf does not wither. Whatever he does prospers (vs. 1-3).

We notice that the person who wrote this Psalm did not take a cursory interest in God's Word. He delighted in feeding himself from it both day and night. He meditated on God's Word, or mulled it over in his mind as a cow chews its cud. As the psalmist contemplated God's Word and his mind dwelled on truth, he is pictured as a luxuriant, fruit-bearing tree. Isn't this what you and I desire for our lives?

Just as a tree is always growing, our knowledge of God and our longing for Him should always be growing. We grow in our relationship with the Lord and know Him more intimately as the affections of our life are absorbed in seeking Him. Knowing God is a continual way of life and the path of joy.

As we read the following prayer from the book, *The Valley of Vision: A Collection of Puritan Prayers & Devotions*, may it express our longing to know the Lord and enjoy greater intimacy with Him:

LONGINGS AFTER GOD

My dear Lord,
I can but tell thee that thou knowest
    I long for nothing but thyself
        nothing but holiness
        nothing but union with thy will.
Thou hast given me these desires
    and thou alone canst give me the thing desired.
My soul longs for communion with thee,
    for mortification of indwelling corruption,

especially spiritual pride.
How precious it is
to have a tender sense and clear apprehension
of the mystery of godliness,
of true holiness!
What a blessedness to be like thee
as much as it is possible for a creature to be like
its creator!
Lord, give me more of thy likeness;
Enlarge me to live more for thee.
Help me to be less pleased with my spiritual experiences,
and when I feel at ease after sweet communings,
teach me it is far too little I know and do.
Blessed Lord,
let me climb up near to thee,
and love, and long, and plead, and wrestle with thee,
and pant for deliverance from the body of sin,
for my heart is wandering and lifeless,
and my soul mourns to think
it should ever lose sight of its beloved.
Wrap my life in divine love,
and keep me ever desiring thee,
always humble and resigned to thy will,
more fixed on thyself,
that I may be more fitted for doing and suffering.[9]

Responding to God's Word

1. How would you explain the difference between knowing information about God and personally knowing God?

2. Look up the following verses. What does God say about knowing Him?

   Jeremiah 9:23-24

   Hosea 6:3

   Hosea 6:6

   2 Peter 3:18

3. Read Matthew 22:37. Why is loving God so important to Him? How would you explain the connection between knowing God, loving Him, and enjoying Him? How can you cultivate a deeper love for the Lord and a greater joy in Him?

4. What false ideas do people have about God? Can you think of any false ideas you have had about God? Why is it important to align your mind with the truth of His Word?

5. Can you identify with Mindy? Why or why not?

6. How do you think your time in God's Word might change if you viewed meeting with Him like a daughter running to greet her father? Read Psalm 19:7-14 and note the joys and benefits of God's Word.

7. What happens to your relationship with God and your joy in Him if you pursue knowing Him only when you feel like it? Have you fallen into this trap? What did you learn from this chapter that helps you with this?

8. How is loving God and knowing Him both emotional and volitional?

9. Read Psalm 1:1-3. How is God's Word a path of joy? Have you experienced this? Explain.

4

THE JOY OF ABIDING IN CHRIST

When I was expecting our son, Aaron, I thought I knew what to anticipate as a new mother. Since I assumed my baby would sleep all day, I wondered how I would use all my spare time. After discussing my "problem" with my husband, I decided to learn how to play the piano. Dean and I began to shop for a used piano. I also ordered a daily subscription to the newspaper so during my many leisure hours, I could relax and catch up on world events.

Reality hit when our nearly ten pound son was born! Aaron did not sleep all day or all night. If he wasn't crying, he was eating. Thankfully, we hadn't bought a piano. I canceled our newspaper subscription when so many unread newspapers piled up in our family room that it looked like a recycling center! I felt overwhelmed and unprepared for my new role as a mother. I prayed to the Lord for help.

Four months later, my prayer was answered through an invitation I received to join a motherhood group that was sponsored by the hospital where Aaron was born. I was invited to meet at a woman's home with several other women and their new babies. At our first meeting, my new friends and I shared the struggles and stresses of new motherhood amid much laughter. Our original six-week commitment to get together stretched into years.

As I look back on that time, I have many fond memories of meeting with my motherhood group. I think one of the main reasons we enjoyed getting together is because we all identified with each other. Yet as closely as we related to one another, we couldn't perfectly identify with each other.

Jesus, however, perfectly identifies with you and me. He is the best Friend we could ever have. He understood my fatigue as I mumbled to myself on many sleepless nights, *Nobody ever died from lack of sleep.* He understood my fear when Aaron's temperature soared to 106 degrees. He understood it all because He made me, He made my baby, and He was with me every moment.

When Jesus was on earth, His disciples also looked to Jesus as their best Friend. Jesus showed compassion for Matthew and his outcast friends when He ate dinner at Matthew's home (Matt. 9:10). Jesus comforted John by letting him lean against His chest (John 13:23 NASB). After Jesus' disciples recovered from their initial shock of seeing Him walk on water, Jesus encouraged them with His presence (John 6:16-21). Jesus spent many hours teaching His disciples and giving them His love, comfort, guidance, and encouragement. Jesus' friendship was a constant source of joy for His disciples.

JESUS INTRODUCES THE HELPER

Imagine, then, the shock and grief that must have rippled through the bewildered disciples when Jesus announced He was leaving them. "My children, I will be with you only a little longer" (John 13:33).

How could their best Friend possibly leave them? After all, Matthew had given up a promising career as a tax collector to follow Jesus (Matt. 9:9). Peter and Andrew had left their fishing business for Jesus (Matt. 4:20). His disciples had left everything behind to follow Him. And Jesus was going to leave them? How could this be?

We can imagine the thoughts that may have raced through the minds of Jesus' disciples: *Lord, this wasn't part of the plan. Who will we turn to if You leave us? How can we live or ever experience any joy again without You?*

Jesus, fully aware of their confusion and fear, reassured His men of His everlasting love and friendship. Although He was leaving them, the relationship they enjoyed with Him would never end. Jesus said, "I will ask the Father, and He will give you another Helper, that He may be with you forever; that is the Spirit of truth, whom the world cannot receive, because it does not behold Him or know Him, but you know Him because He abides with you, and will be in you. I will not leave you as orphans; I will come to you" (John 14:16-18 NASB).

If the disciples were confused when Jesus said He was leaving, His words about the Helper must have left them even more perplexed. How could they make sense out of Jesus' puzzling promise that He wouldn't leave them as orphans, even though He was leaving them? How could Jesus come to them if He were gone?

The Lord encouraged His men by telling them it was to their

advantage for Him to leave. Jesus said, "But I tell you the truth, it is to your advantage that I go away; for if I do not go away, the Helper shall not come to you; but if I go, I will send Him to you" (John 16:7 NASB).

Jesus' men, no doubt, grappled to understand how Jesus' departure could possibly help them. The One they loved was going away, and this would somehow benefit them? Can you imagine holding the hand of your loved one who is dying and hearing him say you are better off without him?

The Lord patiently explained to His men that after He departed, He would come to them through the Helper or Holy Spirit. Jesus wouldn't be with them some of the time, but through the Helper they would have the presence of Jesus in them all the time.

Jesus is not the Holy Spirit, but His presence would dwell in them, and also in us, through the Holy Spirit, the third Person of the Trinity. Since the day of Pentecost (Acts 2:4), Jesus has manifested His presence through the Helper, who lives within all believers.

JUST LIKE JESUS

When Jesus spoke about "another" Helper, He used the word *allos,* which means "another of the same kind." Jesus comforted His disciples by telling them the Holy Spirit would love, comfort, encourage, and guide them in the same way as He had done. The disciples didn't need to worry about Jesus leaving them as orphans. With the Holy Spirit indwelling them, they would never be separated from the Lord.

The thought of having the Lord's presence continually abiding in them was a foreign idea to the disciples. Jesus' men never assumed they could be with Him all the time. Although they spent much time with Jesus, they were used to being away from Him some of the time.

When Jesus left heaven and came to earth, He took on the limitations of a physical body. Like us, He was in one place at a time. Sometimes Jesus prayed by Himself or He was with a few of His disciples or He sent them out to do ministry without Him.

It never occurred to Jesus' men that He could always be with them—let alone in them. But when Jesus proclaimed the Helper "will be in you," He inaugurated a whole new way of relating to God. The Lord Himself would come and permanently abide within His people.

We can understand Jesus' disciples having a difficult time taking in the full meaning of Jesus words, especially when we consider their deep sorrow over Jesus' impending death. Jesus, looking into the tear-streaked faces of His beloved friends, encouraged His men with the promise that their "grief will turn to joy" (John 16:20).

Just as Jesus encouraged His men, He also encourages us with the joy of His abiding presence to strengthen, encourage, and guide us. In this chapter, we will talk about the joy of abiding in an intimate relationship with Jesus, the best Friend we could ever have. We will learn what it means to abide in an intimate union with Him and how we can practically abide in Him throughout our day.

AN INTIMATE UNION

To help His men, and us, get a picture of what it means to abide in Him, Jesus told an allegory. Jesus, the Master Communicator, often used ordinary things to explain extraordinary truth. This was no exception. Jesus used the analogy of a grapevine and its branches to illustrate His intimate union with not only His eleven faithful disciples, but with all those who would become His followers.

Maybe you're in a situation that leaves you feeling much like Jesus' disciples felt on that evening many years ago. Are you hurting? Confused? Discouraged? Jesus tenderly gathered His little flock of men around Him to encourage them with words of comfort. Let's also gather around Jesus and listen to His encouraging words as He speaks to us about the joy of abiding in an intimate relationship of love with Him.

Jesus said,

> "Abide in Me, and I in you. As the branch cannot bear fruit of itself, unless it abides in the vine, so neither can you, unless you abide in Me. I am the vine, you are the branches; he who abides in Me, and I in him, he bears much fruit; for apart from Me you can do nothing....These things I have spoken to you, that My joy may be in you, and that your joy may be made full" (John 15:4,5,11 NASB).

In Jesus' analogy, He compared a relationship of abiding in Him with the relationship of a branch to a grapevine. Although grapevines were, and still are, a common sight in the Middle East, many of us have never seen a grapevine growing out of the ground. In his book, *Secrets of the Vine*, Bruce Wilkinson said we "might think that the vine is a long, trailing limb that sprawls along the trellis. Actually, it's the trunk of the plant that grows out of the ground. Vineyard keepers traditionally keep the vine at waist height—thirty-six to forty two inches."[1] The branches, then, grow out of the vine.

ONE WITH CHRIST

As you and I envision a vine and its branches, we see a picture of our relationship with the Lord. If we were to look at a grapevine and its branches, one of the first things we might observe is they are united together as one. The vine and branch are so intimately intertwined that we can't say for sure where one ends and the other begins.

Just as a vine and branch are united together as one, so we are united together as one with the Lord. "But he who unites himself with the Lord is one with him in spirit" (1 Cor. 6:17). When God saves us, we are joined or sealed together in an intimate union with the Lord through the Holy Spirit. "Having believed, you were marked in him with a seal, the promised Holy Spirit" (Eph. 1:13).

The oneness of our relationship with Jesus is illustrated through His words: "Abide in Me, and I in you" (John 15:4 NASB). To abide in Christ and to have Him abide in us means we are joined together with Him in an inseparable union. Apart from the Trinity, there is no more intimate union than our relationship with Jesus. The vine and branches beautifully picture our union of love with Him. Being a Christian isn't Jesus *and* us, but the joy of Jesus *in* us (Rom. 8:9; 1 John 5:12).

I remember after my daughter was born, my difficulty in deciding on a name for her helped me to reflect on the joy of my union with the Lord. When the hospital volunteer brought my daughter's birth certificate into my room, I stared at the space labeled "name" and tried to decide what to write. Whatever I wrote in that space would be my daughter's legal name.

When the volunteer knocked on the door a second time to see if I'd completed the form, I knew I had to make up my mind. I quickly picked up the pen, wrote *Whitney Ann Carlson,* and signed my name.

As I looked at our two names on the birth certificate, I was struck by the fact that as long as I lived, Whitney would always be my daughter. If she were to get married and change her last name, she would still be my daughter.

Thinking about my relationship with my daughter led me to ponder the reality that I will always be my heavenly Father's daughter. Even death can't separate me from Him, but it will usher me into His presence (Rom. 8:38; Phil. 1:23). As believers, you and I have an everlasting hope and joy because we belong to God. We are "a chosen people...a people belonging to God" (1 Peter 2:9).

I like the way Isaiah said it: "One will say, 'I belong to the LORD'...still another will write on his hand, 'The LORD'S' "(44:5). Although we may not have "belonging to the Lord" stamped on our hand, in our hearts God has branded us *MINE.*

We don't need to worry about the security of our relationship with the Lord. "You belong to Christ; and Christ belongs to God" (1 Cor. 3:23 NASB). The Trinity would have to unravel for us to become separated from Christ.

Our joy and security in the Lord are not dependent on our strength, as branches, to hold onto Him. Our joy and security rest in the strength of Jesus, the vine, to hold onto us. And He has promised to never let us go. Jesus said, "I give them eternal life, and they shall never perish; no one can snatch them out of my hand" (John 10:28).

FOREVER FRIENDS

We didn't attach ourselves to the vine, and we can't detach ourselves from the vine. As branches, we are firmly placed in the vine by God Himself, and that is where we will always remain. "It is because of him that you are in Christ Jesus" (1 Cor. 1:30). Nothing can separate us "from the love of God that is in Christ Jesus our Lord" (Rom. 8:39), or the joy that is available to us as we abide in Him.

I remember lying sick in bed on my wedding anniversary and

being encouraged as I thought about the joy of my relationship of abiding in Jesus. I wrote in my journal:

> Lord, You know I've been sick for the last five days. As I lie in bed right now with a fever, I feel detached from life—like it's passing me by. I can hear Dean and the kids laughing in the pool. The flowers sit by the front door one more day, waiting to be planted.
>
> Yet I thank You, Lord, that no matter how I feel or what happens, nothing can separate us from one another. Although I feel like I'm detached from life, what a joy to know I will never be detached from *Your* life. We are forever friends.

Although circumstances in life change, the one invariable we can count on is the Lord's unchanging love for you and me. "A friend loves at all times" (Prov. 17:17). Jesus is our abiding Friend who loves us all the time.

Are you going through a difficult time? Jesus, your best Friend, holds you up and supports you as a vine holds up the branch. You have a Friend who will never leave you or forsake you (Heb.13:5), who loves you forever (Jer. 31:3), and who always does what is best (Rom. 8:28).

Jesus said, "I no longer call you servants, because a servant does not know his master's business. Instead, *I have called you friends*, for everything that I have learned from my Father I have made known to you" (John 15:15 emphasis added). We are not just servants of the Lord, but we are also His friends, His confidants. Jesus' abiding friendship is a constant source of joy and strength for you and me. Andrew Murray said, "Where does the strength of so many believers come from? It comes from the joy of a personal friendship with Jesus."[2]

ABIDING IN THE PERSON OF CHRIST

Jesus talked about His personal friendship with us within the context of abiding in Him. He said, "Abide in Me, and I in you" (John 15:4 NASB). The word *abide* means "to continue, remain, cling to." To abide in Jesus and for Him to abide in us speaks of a relationship of residing or settling down together. Abiding means being at home with Jesus and His being at home with us. To abide in Christ is to remain or continue in an intimate relationship of love with Him. J. Oswald Sanders said abiding is "keeping unbroken contact with Christ in a union of intimate love."[3]

We might wonder why Jesus tells us to remain or abide in Him, since the Bible clearly states that believers will always remain in Jesus. The marriage relationship between a husband and wife might help to illustrate this. When a man and woman say their marriage vows, they pledge to remain or abide together as husband and wife. Many marriages, however, are characterized by husbands and wives who remain together but practically live as though they are apart.

For instance, the husband may come home from work, mutter a few words to his wife, and spend the rest of the evening in front of the television. Or the wife may be preoccupied with the children, housework, her job, and various activities. Although the husband and wife live together, they are not practically abiding together and enjoying an intimate relationship of love.

When we say, "I do," to Jesus and surrender our lives to Him, we are joined together in an intimate union with Him. But some of us go through our day and live as though we are apart from Him. We get up in the morning and immediately start on our list of things we need to accomplish. Our conversations with the Lord during the course of the day are shallow and infrequent. Our enjoyment of Him is equally shallow and infrequent. We rush through our day, fall into bed at night, and begin the same cycle the next morning. Frustrated and discouraged, we wonder, *Where's the joy?*

Jesus doesn't give us a list of ten things we must do to break the cycle. He simply cuts through to the heart of the matter with His words: "Abide in Me" (John 15:4 NASB).

By telling us to abide in Him, it's as if Jesus is saying, "Don't live as though you are apart from Me. Talk to Me, depend on Me, cling to Me, continually be aware of My presence. Don't let anything come between us and hinder the joy of our communion with one another. Remain in Me and enjoy my friendship."

Regarding our relationship of abiding in Jesus, Bruce Wilkinson said,

> Abiding is all about the most important friendship of your life....In abiding, you seek, long for, thirst for, wait for, see, know, love, hear, and respond to...*a person*....
>
> In our Western-style rush to do and perform for God, we often falter at the task of simply enjoying His company. Yet we were created to be dissatisfied and incomplete with less. In the words of the psalmist, "As the deer pants for the water brooks, so pants my soul for You, O God" (Ps. 42:1 author's emphasis).[4]

Jesus doesn't tell us to abide in a plan, program, or denomination. We abide in the *Person* of Jesus Christ. He said, "Abide in *Me*."

Abiding in Jesus is all about cultivating and enjoying an intimate friendship with the living Christ. As we abide in Jesus, our relationship with Him blossoms and grows. Just as a branch clings to the vine, we abide in the Lord as we continually cling to Him in an intimate union of love and friendship.

Are you enjoying your friendship with the Lord? Take a close look at your relationship with Him. Are you truly abiding in Him, or are you abiding in what you do for Him?

A FRIEND OF THE KING

How do you think you would respond if the President sought a friendship with you? Imagine answering your telephone and hearing a man say, "This is the President of the United States. I would like to spend the afternoon with you. Will you accept my invitation?"

At first you laugh as you try to figure out who is playing a joke on you. But it's no joke. It's the real thing.

You stop laughing. The telephone shakes in your trembling hand. The President waits for your response.

"Uh, yes, Mr. President," you finally stammer, "I would be delighted to join you. Thank you for your invitation."

While the thought of spending the afternoon with the President may seem exciting, it doesn't compare to the joy of abiding in Jesus. In Isaiah, we read this about the Lord:

> Surely the nations are like a drop in the bucket; they are regarded as dust on the scales; he weighs the islands as though they were fine sand. "To whom will you compare me? Or who is my equal?" says the Holy One (40:15,25).

This Almighty King is the One who says to you and me, "Abide in Me" (John 15:4 NASB). The staggering realization is this: the King of the universe invites us to enjoy His friendship—not for an afternoon, but every minute of every day forever! He isn't lonely or in need of anything. He is the self-sufficient God who was just fine before we came along.

He *wants* us.

Jesus wants us to know Him, to depend on Him, to enjoy Him, to call Him our best Friend. The Lord Jesus Christ has given you and me the incomprehensible joy of sharing *in His life.* Charles Spurgeon said, "You are the beloved of the Lord and a friend of the Son of God! Kings might well be willing to give up their crowns if they could have such bliss as this."[5]

A TWO-WAY RELATIONSHIP

Our friendship with the Lord isn't one-sided, or it wouldn't be a true friendship. Jesus has given us the joy of having an active role in our friendship with Him. *Abide* is a verb, an action word. Branches don't passively hang off the vine. The natural function of the branch is to actively depend on the vine for its life and nourishment. The branch draws its strength from the vine as its sap flows through the branch.

Our natural function, as believers, is to abide in Christ. Just as a branch depends on the vine, so we must depend on the Lord for all we need to grow and thrive. As we rely on Him, His life and joy flow through us. "The LORD is my strength and my shield; my heart trusts in him, and I am helped. My heart leaps for joy and I will give thanks to him in song" (Ps. 28:7).

God the Father has brought us into a union of abiding in His Son, but we make decisions throughout our day that practically determine whether we experience the joy of abiding in Him. Oswald Chambers said, "Our Lord did not say, 'Ask God that you may abide in Me;' He said, 'Abide in me,' it is something we have to do."[6] The Lord will guide, comfort, strengthen, and encourage us *as* we choose to rely on Him.

For example, my friend, Karen, (name changed) called me one day, and we started to talk about abiding. Karen had just returned from a long vacation. She mentioned that while she was on vacation, she had been so busy that she hadn't given much thought to the Lord. Upon returning from her trip, she felt depleted.

As we talked about abiding in the Lord, she exclaimed, "We make choices, don't we? I'm united to Jesus like a branch is connected to the vine, but I was living like I wasn't. That's why I feel so disconnected!"

As Karen discovered, abiding in the Lord doesn't just happen. Abiding requires thought and intentionality. We intentionally abide in Jesus as we make choices to spend time in His Word, pray, and to be consciously aware of His presence as we go about our day.

A branch doesn't go for a few days or weeks and not draw its life from the vine. It would wither. The branch abides in the vine moment-by-moment each day. How do you think Karen could practically abide in the Lord and be conscious of His presence the next time she goes on vacation?

HE IS THERE

You and I become more aware of Jesus' presence as we actively choose to abide in Him in the daily matters of life. Whatever our phase of life, and in whatever circumstances we find ourselves, we want to remind ourselves that we are in the presence of Jesus. Whether we are single, married, young, old, running errands, at work, at home, on vacation, sick or well, in times of war or peace—whatever we're doing and wherever we are...Jesus is there.

Are you and I aware of His presence and enjoying Him? Andrew Murray said, "The secret of the Christian's strength and joy is simply the presence of the Lord Jesus."[7] To abide in Christ is a day-by-day, moment-by-moment consciousness of His presence and reliance upon His Person that results in greater joy and intimacy with Him.

How do we practically abide in our friendship with Jesus? How do we train ourselves to become more mindful of Him and know the joy of His presence?

I find that being thankful for little things helps me to develop a greater awareness of Jesus' presence. As I brush my teeth, I think about how glad I am to have a toothbrush and toothpaste. I thank Him for running water that is safe to drink and a hot shower.

From there, your list and mine can go on to include the many things God gives us. As we remember to thank the Lord as we go through our day, we practically abide in Him and increase our joy as we become more aware of His goodness. How else do you think we can become more aware of Jesus' presence?

PRACTICING HIS PRESENCE

Martyn Lloyd-Jones gives this helpful recommendation on how to be mindful of the Lord's presence from the moment we wake up:

> When I wake up in the morning, before I allow myself to think about anything else, I say to myself, "You are a child of God and an heir of eternity; God knows you and you belong to Him"—recollection! Now, I must do that, and do it forcibly, because the moment I wake up thoughts will come crowding into my mind, perhaps temptations, perhaps doubts; all sorts of things. But I brush them all aside and deliberately remind myself of God and myself and my relationship to Him. And I meditate upon that and then I consciously seek the presence

> of God. To put it another way, I must "practice the presence of God."
>
> In other words, I say to myself, God is and I am, and God is there. God is eternal being and life and reality. He is not a mere term or a philosophical concept—God *is.* He is a Person, and I want to go into His presence. I want to know Him; I want to speak to Him. I am going to approach Him, as I may decide to visit a friend. I am going to visit God and commune with Him; I am going to have fellowship with Him (author's emphasis).[8]

Let's say, however, we neglect to start our morning as Dr. Lloyd-Jones recommends. As the day goes on and our pressures increase, we feel frustrated and unfocused. How do we get back to consciously abiding in Christ and enjoying His presence when we've become anxious and worried?

I asked my friend, Laura, if she would write down how abiding in Christ has practically changed her life—especially as she faces her daily stresses. When we met for lunch, she handed me a yellow, legal-size sheet of paper that was filled front and back. Laura wrote:

> I wanted to experience victory in the day-to-day pressures of life, but I often felt worried and anxious. I was really struggling with anxiety as I planned my son's second birthday party. At one point, I found myself standing in my kitchen completely confused. Then I got down on my knees and said, "God, why am I so worried? Help me through my mental confusion."
>
> God showed me why I was so anxious. I was trying to put together the party on my own—without consciously abiding in the Lord and relying on Him. When I realized

this and relied on the Lord, I experienced self-control over my anxiety, and I was able to enjoy Richie's birthday party.

My worry over Richie's party was just an example of the anxiety and fear in my life. I felt frustrated at not being able to experience peace, joy, and self-control in my daily pressures as I desired. But God showed me I was trying to put together not only Richie's party, but many aspects of my life in my own strength.

As I've been intentionally abiding in Christ, I've seen my life change. Areas of my life that lacked control are getting under control, and I have peace and joy. Some of the ways I intentionally abide in the Lord throughout my day are by reading my Bible, praying, listening to great pastors preach on the radio, and having a mature Christian in my life who is strong in her relationship with the Lord. These things have helped me to grow in Christ and expand my knowledge of Him.

Abiding in Christ has made a major, practical difference in my life. I realize I need to put God first and have a daily consciousness of Him if I am going to experience victory in the pressures of life. I must focus on who God is and seek Him in order to be the woman He wants me to be. Abiding in Christ is setting my entire mind on Him and having all-consuming thoughts of Him. I believe abiding in Christ *is* the Christian life and needs to be taken seriously (Laura's emphasis).

THE JOY OF CHILDLIKE DEPENDENCY

Laura said, "Abiding in Christ *is* the Christian life." She is right. We often make abiding so much more complicated than it is. Situations in life might be complicated, but abiding in Christ is not. Abiding may not always be easy, but it is not complex.

Just as we come into the kingdom through childlike faith—in complete dependence upon the Lord, realizing we have nothing—so we continue in childlike dependence upon the Lord—realizing we can do nothing apart from Him. Jesus reminds us: "Apart from Me you can do nothing," (John 15:5). Apart from relying on Him, we can do nothing of eternal significance. In fact, as Laura said, if we're not abiding in the Lord moment-by-moment, we may get discouraged and confused when we're planning a birthday party!

As a child grows up, he leaves his mother's arms and depends on himself to take care of his needs. In contrast, we grow up spiritually as we remain in Jesus' arms and maintain a childlike reliance upon Him. A relationship of abiding in Jesus is characterized by greater dependence on Him and less dependence on ourselves. John the Baptist said, "He must become greater; I must become less" (John 3:30). Christ-reliance must increase, and self-reliance must decrease.

We are to grow up in the Lord and not be childish, but we are never to lose our childlike dependency upon Him. Spiritual growth is seen by an increasing awareness of our inability to do anything apart from His ability. In childlike reliance upon the Lord, we discover the joy of abiding in Him.

Sometimes, however, don't we think we can handle things on our own? Instead of abiding close to Jesus and enjoying His presence, we jump away from Him. But in doing this, we inhibit the joy of simply abiding in Him as a baby abides in the arms of his mother. What can a baby do apart from depending on the care of his parents? Nothing but make a mess. In our own strength, apart from Jesus, all you and I can do is make a mess.

Most of us wouldn't consciously think, *I'm not going to abide in the Lord today. I'm going to do things on my own.* We just forget to be mindful of Him; we forget to pray; we forget to seek His wisdom before we make decisions. Because the Lord wants us to depend on Him and enjoy His friendship, He often puts us in situations where we come face-to-face with our weaknesses.

A couple of days after I had surgery, I had to face a physical limitation. A nurse walked into my room, unhooked me from the machine I was connected to, and announced I could walk to the bathroom by myself. I thought, *How can I possibly do that?*

I was in the bed by the window, and the fifteen feet to the bathroom looked like miles. I prayed to the Lord for strength. Then I gingerly stepped out of bed and slowly made my way to the bathroom. I made it there and back with pain, but no other problems. As I lay back in bed, I breathed a sigh of relief and a prayer of thanks to the Lord.

Unless we have a physical limitation, we probably don't pray for the strength to walk across the room every time we stand up. We can do it on our own. Sometimes we walk through our day with a similar attitude: we think we can handle things ourselves. Has the Lord recently brought you face-to-face with a situation you thought you could handle, but then you discovered you couldn't? What are you learning through this?

For us to know the joy of abiding in Christ, we need to humbly admit our weaknesses and acknowledge that apart from Him, we can do absolutely nothing. When Jesus said, "Apart from Me you can do nothing," that's exactly what He meant (John 15:5). As various situations arise during our day, we need to remind ourselves that we are connected to Jesus, and we desperately need to abide in Him.

You and I practically live in and experience the joy of our friendship with the Lord as we continually look to Him for all we need. Let's pray that the Lord will show us how much we need to closely abide in Him. Let's ask Him to show us how we can become more aware of His presence throughout our day and know the joy of abiding in Jesus, our best Friend.

Responding to God's Word

1. What do the following verses say about the believer's eternal security in Christ? How does this encourage you?

   John 6:39

   John 10:27-28

   Romans 8:38-39

   Hebrews 7:25

2. List some of the things you do to cultivate a relationship with a friend.

   How can you incorporate these things into your friendship with Jesus?

3. What qualities do you appreciate and enjoy about a good friend?

   What do you appreciate and enjoy about Jesus? Write Him a thank you note of appreciation.

   Dear Jesus,

4. What does it mean to abide in Christ? How does Jesus' analogy of the vine and branches illustrate this? What is the relationship between abiding in Christ and experiencing joy?

5. How can you relate to Karen or Laura? How can a person be united to Jesus, the vine, yet not experience the joy of that union?

6. Andrew Murray said, "The secret of the Christian's strength and joy is simply the presence of the Lord Jesus." Think of ways you can intentionally abide in the Lord and become more aware of His presence.

   How can you specifically put this into practice this week?

7. Can you think of a situation you thought you could handle on you own, but then discovered you couldn't? What did God show you?

8. How does depending on Jesus through simple, childlike trust become a path of joy?

9. What are you depending on the Lord for in the following areas (where applicable):

   Yourself

   Marriage

   Children

   Job

   Ministry outside your home

5

THE FRUIT OF JOY

We have two big apple trees planted in our side yard. Earlier this spring the trees were covered with fragrant, pink blossoms. Now the trees are laden with little, green apples. When my husband mows the grass, he has to nearly crawl under the trees because the branches are loaded with so much fruit. This fall, I anticipate picking many apples to eat fresh and make into applesauce.

Just as our apple trees are filled with fruit, so our lives as Christians are to be filled with the fruit of the Spirit. Who among us doesn't yearn to have a fruit-filled life? Don't we long for lives that, like the branches of an apple tree, are laden with much fruit? In this chapter, we will see how the Holy Spirit produces fruit in us, specifically the fruit of joy, as we abide in Christ.

WHAT IS FRUIT?

Let's start by asking the question, "What is fruit?" Fruit is the outward evidence of our inward condition. Fruit shows us, and those who come in contact with us, what we're made of inside.

In the Bible, the word *fruit* is used both negatively and positively to describe the manifestation of what is in a person's heart. For example, Jesus said,

> "No good tree bears bad fruit, nor does a bad tree bear good fruit. Each tree is recognized by its own fruit. People do not pick figs from thornbushes, or grapes from briers. The good man brings good things out of the good stored up in his heart, and the evil man brings evil things out of the evil stored up in his heart. For out of the overflow of his heart the mouth speaks" (Luke 6:43-45).

All of us give evidence of what is within us, whether good or bad, by the fruit we bear. Fruit reveals our true nature. Fruit is the overflow, or by-product, of what we have stored in our hearts.

We can know what is in our hearts by looking at the fruit of our lives. A good tree will bear rich, luscious fruit that is a joy to behold. In contrast, a bad tree will bear rotten fruit that is smelly and repugnant.

The Apostle Paul contrasted bad fruit, or the deeds of the flesh, with the fruit of the Spirit. In Galatians 5:19-23, we see what these negative and positive fruit are:

> The acts of the sinful nature are obvious: sexual immorality, impurity and debauchery; idolatry and witchcraft; hatred, discord, jealousy, fits of rage, selfish ambition, dissensions, factions and envy; drunkenness, orgies, and the like. I warn you, as I did before, that those who

> live like this will not inherit the kingdom of God.
>
> But the fruit of the Spirit is love, joy, peace, patience, kindness, goodness, faithfulness, gentleness and self-control. Against such things there is no law.

Let's read these verses again and take an inventory of our lives. What do we struggle with on the first list? What do we desire to see more of in our lives from Paul's second list? How do we bear fruit of the Spirit?

OUR COMMANDMENTS

Maybe we think to ourselves, *I know what I need to do to bear fruit. I'll work harder.* Then we make up our own commandments on how to bear such fruit as love, joy, peace, and patience. Our commandments go something like this:

> I will work hard to love the person I can't stand.
> I will try to be joyful, even if it kills me.
> I will have peace, I will have peace, I will have peace.
> I will be patient or have a heart attack.

We muster up all the strength we have and try as hard as we can to produce fruit. But we fail. So we determine to work harder. Once again, we give it our best shot. And again, we fail.

Then, in desperation, we say to God, "You know how hard I'm working to get more love, joy, and peace in my life. I'm trying to be patient about this, but I can't wait much longer!"

Have you ever tried to keep your own commandments in an effort to bear fruit? I have. I used to lack self-control to get to bed on time. I would stay up and watch the news. Then after the news, I might decide to bake cookies. Some people do fine on little sleep. I am not one of them.

Like weeds in a garden, my lack of self-control at night caused problems to sprout up during the day. I felt like I was in a fog and had a hard time concentrating. In an attempt to remedy my problem, I made a sign and hung it on the inside of the medicine cabinet. My sign said "Be in bed by 10:45."

I tried to obey my sign and get the self-control I desired, but I repeatedly failed. As I was praying about this one day, God gave me the perspective I needed. He showed me this area of my life was not under the control of the Holy Spirit. I needed to yield myself to the Lord and depend on Him to produce the fruit of self-control.

When faced with the nightly temptation to stay up, instead of trying to obey what I had written, I obeyed what God had written—specifically this verse: "I delight to do Your will, O my God, And Your law is within my heart" (Ps. 40:8 NKJV). Rather than focusing on my outward law, I remembered the inward law of God. As I relied on the Lord, He produced the fruit of self-control in my life. And that was a joy!

A fruitful life is not something we achieve through our efforts to adhere to our self-imposed commandments or laws. The Apostle Paul said there is no law against the fruit of the Spirit (Gal. 5:23). In other words, no outside law or regulation can produce fruit, because fruit is produced by the Spirit.

In Galatians, the same book in which we find the fruit of the Spirit, Paul said, "Are you so foolish? After beginning with the Spirit, are you now trying to attain your goal by human effort?" (3:3). It is impossible for us to bear the fruit of the Sprit through our self-efforts. If we could produce fruit through our human efforts, fruit would no longer be of the Spirit. Then we would receive the glory for what we produce, instead of God.

A SINGULAR SOURCE OF FRUIT

Instead of imposing rules on ourselves, maybe we think the way to have a fruit-filled life is to ask God to give us whatever fruit we think we're lacking. For instance, when we encounter a difficult person, we plead with God saying, "Pleeease give me love for this person!" When we're impatient, we ask for the fruit of patience. When we eat too much, we ask God for the fruit of self-control.

We pray for an appropriate fruit to match each circumstance or stress in our lives. This process of asking God for situational fruit becomes a wearisome cycle. We inevitably become upset with ourselves when we once again have a bad attitude toward someone, or we're impatient, or we eat too much. Our frustration adversely affects our peace and joy, which we then pray God will increase.

Asking God to give us fruit, as though fruit were a commodity, is not the path to a fruitful life. How we often compartmentalize the fruit of the Spirit like pieces of fruit we find in the produce section at the grocery store. We ask God to give us love, joy, peace, and patience as though these fruit are like bananas, oranges, apples, and grapes!

God doesn't give us pieces of fruit here-and-there. When Paul wrote to the Galatians, he referred to the *fruit* of the Spirit, rather than the *fruits* of the Spirit (5:22). This singular use of the word *fruit* is important because it shows us that fruit of the Spirit are not individual items. It also shows us that fruit is produced through a singular source—the Holy Spirit. "For the kingdom of God is...righteousness, peace and joy in the Holy Spirit" (Rom. 14:17).

Instead of giving us individual pieces of fruit, God has given us an Individual—His Son. We have the all-sufficient Christ living within us. He abides in us through the Holy Spirit who reveals to us all we have through Christ Jesus our Lord. Now let's see how the Holy Spirit actually produces fruit in us. What is key to experiencing the joy of a fruitful life?

THE SUFFICIENCY OF JESUS

The Holy Spirit produces fruit in us as we yield ourselves to Jesus. The key to a fruit-filled life is to abide in Jesus and become like Him.

In John 15, we find the inherent relationship between abiding in Jesus and bearing fruit:

> "Abide in Me, and I in you. As the branch cannot bear fruit of itself, unless it abides in the vine, so neither can you, unless you abide in Me. I am the vine, you are the branches; he who abides in Me, and I in him, he bears much fruit; for apart from Me you can do nothing" (vs. 4-5 NASB).

Jesus reminds us of what we are: branches. Simple objects. The beauty of Jesus' allegory of the vine and branches is in its magnificent simplicity. We are branches whose sole purpose and aim in life is to abide in Christ and glorify Him through bearing much fruit.

Jesus also states what may seem obvious: "The branch cannot bear fruit of itself, unless it abides in the vine" (John 15:4 NASB). No one would ever think a branch of a grapevine could bear fruit by itself, apart from receiving the life-giving sap of the vine. Why would Jesus talk about something that seems so apparent?

It's because He knows us. He knows our inclination to rely on ourselves instead of Him. Jesus said, "Neither can you [bear fruit], unless you abide in Me" (John 15:4 NASB).

Although you and I are incapable of producing a puny raisin in our own strength, nevertheless, some of us put incredible pressure on ourselves to try to produce fruit. Imagine what a branch might say if it thought it had the responsibility to produce fruit:

> "I never knew being a branch could be so hard. Am I bearing enough fruit? What is the quality of my fruit? What do the other branches think of my fruit? I've tried fertilizers that promise an abundant crop, and I've read books and attended seminars that guarantee fruit in three easy steps. What do I have? Plastic fruit!"

If we're feeling depleted, we need to ask ourselves some questions: Do I think everything depends on me? Do I feel like I'm carrying the weight of the world? Must I know all the answers, or will I be content to trust Jesus?

If our joy seems like a memory, it could be we're trying to *be* the vine, rather than abiding *in* the vine. Sometimes we get our part, as branches, mixed up with Jesus' part, as the vine. This is not the path of joy, but a sure way of becoming spiritually, emotionally, and physically drained. The Christian life becomes a heavy load if we think everything depends on us.

The good news is that everything depends on Jesus, not us! The path to a fruit-filled life is not through us concentrating on bearing fruit, but by us concentrating on Jesus and becoming more like Him. Jesus clearly tells us we cannot bear fruit apart from Him, because fruit is *of* the Spirit. It's *His* crop. Not ours.

We experience the power of Jesus' life in us as we rely on Him—not ourselves or other branches. When we realize who we are—simple branches who desperately need the nourishing life-sap of Jesus flowing through us—we truly live the Christian life.

Abiding in Jesus is the path of joy because it takes the pressure off us to produce fruit, which we can't do anyway.

ALL THINGS THROUGH CHRIST

Just as our self-efforts were of no avail to save us, so our self-efforts to grind out fruit are equally futile. But this doesn't mean we have no part in the fruit bearing process. While Jesus reminds us, "Apart from Me you can do nothing," (John 15:5) the Apostle Paul said, "I can do everything through him who gives me strength" (Phil. 4:13). In ourselves, apart from relying on the Lord, we can do nothing. But we can do all things as we abide in Christ who supplies us with His strength and power.

The Holy Spirit produces fruit in us (His part) as we abide in the Lord and receive our strength from Him (our part) to bear fruit. The vine and the branches have different functions, but both work together as one.

Martyn Lloyd-Jones cxplains how this works:

> The Christian life is not a life that I live myself and by my own power; neither is it a life in which I am obliterated and Christ does all. No, "I can do all things through Christ...."
>
> Do not agonize in prayer beseeching Him for power. Do what He has told you to do. Live the Christian life. Pray, and meditate upon Him. Spend time with Him and ask Him to manifest Himself to you. And as long as you do that you can leave the rest to Him.[1]

BECOMING LIKE JESUS

As we yield ourselves to the Lord, we are filled with the fruit of His righteous life. In Philippians 1:11, Paul talked about believers being "filled with the fruit of righteousness that comes through

Jesus Christ—to the glory and praise of God." As Paul pointed out, fruit "comes through Jesus Christ." When we are filled with Him, we are filled with the fruit of His life. Fruit is the spillover of a life filled with Christ. In order for us to have fruit-filled lives, we abide closely in Jesus and focus on becoming like Him.

As we become more like Him, the evidence of His righteous life is manifested in us as fruit. He is perfect love, full joy, the Prince of peace, patient, kind, good, faithful, gentle, and self-controlled (Ex. 34:6; John 15:11; Is. 9:6; Ps. 89:1). We have the source and producer of fruit living within us. This is why we don't need to ask God to give us more fruit. He has already given us all we need in His Son. What we need to do is to become more like Jesus.

As we abide in our intimate union with Jesus, we begin to look like Him—loving, joyful, peaceful, patient, and so on. Our resemblance to Jesus is manifested as fruit of the Spirit. Fruit is the outward evidence of a close, inner walk with the Lord. As we rely on Him, the Holy Spirit reproduces the likeness of Christ in us. As we live in conscious awareness of His presence, His life flows through us, energizing and empowering us to bear fruit.

The fruit of joy, along with all the fruit of the Spirit, is the nature of Christ reproduced in us as we abide in Him (2 Cor. 3:18). Oswald Chambers put it like this: "Joy is neither happiness or brightness, joy is the nature of God in my blood, no matter what happens."[2] Joy is the overflow of Jesus' life in us. We don't aim at getting the fruit of joy; we aim at becoming like Jesus.

The closer we abide in Jesus, the more we become like Him. The more we become like Him, the more fruit we bear. The more fruit we bear, the more we glorify God. Jesus said, "By this is My Father glorified, that you bear much fruit, and so prove to be My disciples" (John 15:8 NASB). The more we glorify God by bearing much fruit, the more we please Him.

Think about the pleasure a farmer has as he walks through His vineyard and sees an abundant harvest of rich, luscious grapes. Think of the pleasure we give to our Father when He looks at us and sees the nature of His Son reproduced in us as an abundant harvest of fruit. Joy is the satisfaction of knowing our lives give pleasure to God. Now let's see how we practically experience the joy of a fruitful life. What does this look like in our daily lives?

ABIDING IN HIS LOVE

"Love" heads the list of fruit in Galatians 5:22. We're going to look at the fruit of love and see what it is and how we experience it. We want to remember that this fruit is not produced independently of the other fruit, such as joy. As we become more like the Lord, we bear the fruit of love and joy, along with the other fruit of the Spirit.

In Romans we read: "And hope does not disappoint us, because God has poured out his love into our hearts by the Holy Spirit, whom he has given us" (5:5). God has poured out, or lavished, His love upon us. God has given us all of His love through His Spirit. We, therefore, don't need to ask the Lord for more love (since we already have His complete love), rather we need to walk closely with Him.

Instead of determining to knuckle under and trying to become more loving or begging God to give us love for a difficult person, we abide in the Lord of love. Jesus said, "Just as the Father has loved Me, I have also loved you; abide in My love" (John 15:9 NASB).

Let's read this verse once more. "*Just as* the Father has loved Me, I have also loved you; abide in My love." Jesus' love for you is *just like* the Father's love for Him. Take a moment right now and think of words that describe the Father's love for Jesus. If you have a pen, write down your thoughts.

Now think of those same words as describing Jesus' love for you.

This is the love—*His* love—that Jesus desires you to abide in and give away to others. Immerse yourself in His love, bask in His love, delight in His love, but don't keep such magnificent love to yourself!

Jesus said, "This is My commandment, that you love one another, *just as* I have loved you" (John 15:12 NASB emphasis added). The way we become more loving is by becoming more like Christ and loving others with the love He has for us. As we abide in Him, we bear through Him the fruit or overflow of His love.

We often think of love as a reciprocal emotion. We love people who love us. But anybody can extend love to someone who is friendly and loving in return. Jesus said, "If you love those who love you, what reward will you get? Are not even the tax collectors doing that?" (Matt. 5:46). This is the love of natural human emotion, not a supernatural fruit.

The fruit of love is different from a warm feeling for someone who loves us. Jesus startled His listeners by saying, "But I tell you: Love your enemies and pray for those who persecute you, that you may be sons of your Father in heaven" (Matt. 5:44,45).

It's hard enough for most of us to love people who pull out in front of us and drive slowly. How can we possibly love irritating, mean people? Apart from abiding in Christ, we can't.

Biblical love is produced by the power of the Holy Spirit, which makes it a supernatural fruit, rather than a natural emotion. This love is God's own love, in us, that reaches out and loves people for whom we may not have loving feelings. As we abide in Christ we abide in His love, and through Him we give His love to undeserving people.

Jesus didn't die for us because we were such wonderful, loving people. We were His enemies—sinners who had greatly offended Him. "But God demonstrates his own love for us in this: While we were still sinners, Christ died for us" (Rom. 5:8). In an act of self-sacrificing love, Jesus showed us how much He loved us from the cross. This self-sacrificing love is what He desires you and me to give away to others as the fruit of His love.

The Joy Of Loving Like Jesus

We might say, "All right, I see how the fruit of love is produced by the Holy Spirit as I rely on Christ to love others with His love, but is there any joy in this?"

Yes! Jesus said, "Blessed [joyful] are you when men hate you, when they exclude you and insult you and reject your name as evil, because of the Son of Man. Rejoice in that day and leap for joy, because great is your reward in heaven. For that is how their fathers treated the prophets" (Luke 6:22-23). Jesus' words had special meaning for His disciples who would soon be persecuted for their faith. In a broader sense, we see from these verses how we should respond whenever we are mistreated.

When Jesus said, "If you love those who love you, what reward will you get?" (Matt. 5:46), the implication is this love has no reward. But when we love those who mistreat us, Jesus promises us a great reward in heaven. He tells us to leap for joy and be glad because we know our reward is coming! As we place our suffering in God's hands, He gives us His supernatural love and joy along this difficult path.

Noreen (name changed) learned how to love with Jesus' love in a situation she would have never thought possible. Noreen never imagined her marriage would be anything but bliss. She thought she had married the man of her dreams.

One day when Noreen was cleaning under the couch, she found a plastic bag filled with pills. When she asked her husband about it, she believed Steve's (name changed) excuse. Why would she doubt him? After all, she was married to Prince Charming.

Then Steve's behavior became increasingly erratic. He lost weight, and she found more pills. In the garage. Stashed in the cupboards. Behind the furniture. Noreen couldn't believe his lies any longer. The truth hit hard.

Steve was a drug addict.

It was at this point that Noreen and I met one another. A few weeks into our budding friendship Noreen called me, sobbing. Steve had been arrested for shoplifting, and the police had found drugs in his car.

Noreen was filled with fear and rage. She told me she was leaving Steve. Since Noreen was in no danger from her husband, I urged her to stay with him. She did.

Noreen and I began to meet together to pray and seek God's wisdom, guidance, and encouragement from His Word. Noreen experienced a breakthrough when she realized that because Jesus loved her and forgave her, she also needed to love Steve with Jesus' love and forgive him. Through the power of God, Noreen forgave the man who had shattered her life.

With the block of unforgiveness removed, God filled her heart with renewed hope and, yes, joy. A genuine love for Steve began to grow within her. The fruit of love. Although Noreen and Steve still had a bumpy road ahead of them, she continued to abide in the Lord. Noreen relied on Him to give her the strength, moment-by-moment, to remain in her marriage and to love her husband with Jesus' love. Steve is now completely free of drugs, and their marriage is restored.

Sometimes when Noreen and I get together, she still cries. But not because she is sad. She shakes her head with wonder and says, "I know my love for Steve was not from me. It was absolutely supernatural. God gave me His eyes, His vision, His heart for Steve. Through Jesus' love for me, I was able to love my husband."

The Joy Of Abiding Through Obeying

Jesus followed His statement on abiding in His love by telling us how we do this. He said, "If you keep My commandments, you will abide in My love; just as I have kept My Father's commandments, and abide in His love" (John 15:10 NASB).

We practically remain in Jesus' love and know His joy by obeying Him. Jesus' joy of abiding in His Father's love by obeying Him is the joy Jesus gives to us as we abide in His love by obeying Him.

When Noreen realized God wanted her to forgive Steve, she didn't jump at the idea. Her flesh wanted to feed the anger. But in her heart, she wanted to obey the Lord. Although Noreen didn't feel like forgiving Steve, she forgave him as an act of obedience unto the Lord.

Noreen proved her love for the Lord by her willingness to obey Him. After Noreen forgave Steve, she experienced Jesus' love for her and the nearness of His presence more intimately. This, in turn, increased her joy, peace, and her ability to be patient and kind with Steve. By abiding in Christ and obeying Him, all the fruit of Jesus' life became increasingly evident in Noreen's life.

Who has hurt you? Who has made your life difficult? Have

you forgiven this person? Unforgiveness hinders us from enjoying a close relationship with Jesus and stunts the fruit of the Spirit from growing. Ephesians 4:32 says, "Be kind and compassionate to one another, forgiving each other, *just as* in Christ God forgave you" (emphasis added). Go before the Lord and forgive this person. Be free from your anger and walk the path of joy unhindered.

Jesus said, "If you love me, you will obey what I command" (John 14:15). Our obedience to Jesus and our subsequent love for others proves we are His true disciples. As we abide in the Lord by obeying Him, He places within us the joy of knowing our obedience pleases Him. Joy is a fruit the Holy Spirit produces in us as we walk by faith in obedience to Christ.

God's Joy In Our Obedience

The Apostle John said, "Our fellowship is with the Father and with His Son, Jesus Christ" (1 John 1:3). How can we enjoy intimate fellowship with Jesus if we are disobeying His Word? How can the Holy Spirit produce the fruit of joy in us if we are grieving Him? All the precepts of our Lord are signposts that direct us to the path of joy. Through obeying His Word, we bring joy to our Lord and practically abide in His love and joy.

I remember how my relationship with our son, Aaron, was strained when he disobeyed me and what pleasure he gave me through his obedience. When Aaron first learned to talk, the word *no* quickly became one of his favorite things to say. It seemed like whenever I asked Aaron to do something, he said, "No."

Although I still loved Aaron when he disobeyed me, on those occasions when he responded, "Yes, Mommy," I felt like someone opened a window and let in a fresh, spring breeze! Maybe God feels like that each time we say to Him, "Yes, Father."

I appreciate what Charles Spurgeon said about the mutual joy we share with the Lord as we obey Him:

> In as much as Jesus Christ can look upon you with joy as obedient and faithful to Him, in that same proportion your conscience will be at ease, and your mind will find joy in the thought that your life is acceptable to Him.
>
> Day by day, if you continue to walk with God carefully and prayerfully and to abide in Christ continually, He will look upon you with eyes of satisfaction and delight. He will see in you the reward of His sufferings. And you, being conscious that you are giving joy to Him, will find that your own cup of joy is also full to overflowing.[3]

A motivation for us to obey the Lord is that we care about how He feels. Oswald Chambers said, "The spirit of obedience gives more joy to God than anything else on earth."[4] God doesn't love us more when we obey Him, but our obedience provides the avenue for joy in both His heart and ours. Obedience is the path to mutual joy with the Lord.

ABIDING IN JESUS' JOY

Following Jesus' instruction on abiding in His love by obeying Him, He said, "These things I have spoken to you, that My joy may be in you, and that your joy may be made full" (John 15:11 NASB). The full joy Jesus spoke of is *His own joy* that He places in us as we abide in Him. Jesus said, "*My* joy may be in you." The more fully we abide in Him, we more fully we experience the fruit of His joy. Jesus invites us, urges us, commands us to abide in Him so we will be filled with His joy and bring glory to God for the fruit He produces in us.

I like what Bible commentator R.C.H. Lenski said about the fruit of joy:

> This [joy] is not a fatuous joy such as the world accepts; it is the enduring joy that bubbles up from all the grace of God in our possession, from the blessedness that is ours, that is undimmed by tribulation, that merges into the joy of heaven. This is the sunshine that ever beams for the believer.[5]

This is the joy that God desires to produce within you and me! The power of the Holy Spirit to produce the fruit of Jesus' full joy is released in us as we abide in Him and are filled with the Holy Spirit. In the book of Acts, we read: "And the disciples were filled with joy and with the Holy Spirit" (13:52). Similarly, Romans 15:13 says, "May the God of hope fill you with all joy and peace as you trust in him, so that you may overflow with hope by the power of the Holy Spirit."

A Spirit-filled heart is a joyful heart. "And do not get drunk with wine, for that is dissipation, but be filled with the Spirit, speaking to one another in psalms and hymns and spiritual songs, singing and making melody in your heart to the Lord" (Eph. 5:18-19 NASB). Dr. Lenski commented on this portion of Scripture by saying,

> It is spiritual joy, happiness, enthusiasm, thankfulness that overflow in the utterance of psalms, hymns and odes even as the mouth speaks from the abundance of the heart....Our spirit is ever to be filled so that it overflows with spiritual expressions.[6]

When our lives are filled with joy, God is glorified because He is displayed as the source of our rejoicing. Joy is the overflow of a life that is filled with the Spirit of joy. Joy is the outward reality of God working within us to make us like His Son. When the Holy Spirit produces the fruit of joy in us, we can't help but splash His joy onto those around us.

OBVIOUS JOY

When I look at our apple trees in September, I see ripe, delicious apples. I don't have to peer under the leaves to search for fruit. It's in plain sight for all to see. Likewise, when we abide in Jesus, others readily see the fruit of His joyful life as it's expressed in our personalities.

Some of us have quiet, easygoing personalities. Others of us are talkative and energetic. The word *joyful* does not describe a type of personality, but the by-product of abiding in Jesus. Joy is not reserved for a certain temperament or disposition. Joy goes beyond personality, yet it should be expressed within our personalities. As we abide in Christ and are filled with Him, God doesn't subvert our personalities; rather we bloom and grow into the fruitful people God intends us to be.

The fruit of joy is displayed in various ways within our personalities. For instance, a Jonathan apple is one kind of apple and a McIntosh is another. They are both apples, but they are not the same kind of apple. In a similar way, the fruit of joy may be expressed differently within our unique personalities.

For example, maybe you tend to be critical and negative. But as you abide closely in Jesus and yield yourself to Him, you become more like Him. Then you express His heart to other people by seeking ways to help and encourage them.

Perhaps you're a complainer. But as you walk by the power of the Holy Spirit and are filled with Him, your complaining gives way to a joyful heart of thanksgiving and praise.

If you're quiet, Jesus' joy may radiate out of you. If you're outgoing, His joy may bubble out. But one way or another, the fruit of His joy is going to come out!

As we become more like Jesus and are filled with His joy, He makes a practical (and wonderful!) difference in our personalities. Other people will notice our joy and benefit from our joy spilling onto them.

A friend told me how she expresses joy by occasionally making fancy dinners for her family. Because of a serious illness, some days she can hardly make dinner at all. So when she serves her family a special meal, they know that's the joy of the Lord flowing onto them.

MY LESSON ON JOY

The Lord used a family vacation to teach me a practical lesson about the joy of abiding in Him. One fall weekend when our kids were younger, we headed to a resort a few hours from our home. I was looking forward to enjoying the brilliant autumn colors and doing some hiking.

As we pulled out of the driveway the sky was blue, the sun was shining, and I was feeling great. But about an hour into our trip, the sky turned dark and it began to rain. Then we listened to the weather forecast for the next day: forty degrees for the high, continued rain, and gusts of high wind. By the time we reached the hotel, my mood was as gray as the sky.

That night as I sat in our hotel room and pouted, I couldn't figure out how Dean could watch a football game on television and Aaron and Whitney could run around the room and play when I was so upset! When I announced I was taking a shower, no one seemed to notice.

As I stood in the shower, I began to pray. God showed me my bad attitude was hindering me from practically abiding in Christ and being filled with Him. I surrendered my attitude and the whole weekend to Him. Then I focused on Jesus and filled my mind with verses of praise, and I took a long, hot shower.

When I finally stepped out of the shower and wrapped myself up in a towel, I saw before me a big, steamy mirror. I was so filled with joy by then, it had to come out. I wrote *I LOVE JESUS!* across the mirror.

The next day our faces turned red from the cold, and our clothes were soaked, but I enjoyed every moment! I kept remembering what I wrote on the mirror. When I, a branch, yielded myself to Jesus, the vine, His joy practically became my joy and was expressed in my personality—much to my family's delight!

When we yield ourselves to Jesus and rely on Him, it makes a practical difference in our lives. Joy isn't something we try to work up. And it isn't dependent on the weather. Joy is a fruit the Holy Spirit produces in us as we abide in Jesus Christ.

Responding to God's Word

1. Read Luke 6:43-45 and Galatians 5:19-23. What is fruit? What does fruit reveal?

2. Can you think of a time when you worked to try to produce spiritual fruit yourself? Was this a joyful experience? Explain.

3. Why does Galatians 5:22 refer to *fruit* of the Spirit rather than *fruits* of the Spirit?

   How are you encouraged to know that God doesn't give us individual pieces of fruit but an Individual, His Son?

4. What is key to having a fruit-filled life? How does bearing much fruit glorify God and bring joy to both God's heart and yours?

5. Examine your life to see if you are trying to *be* the vine rather than abiding *in* the vine: Do you think everything depends on you? Do you feel like you're carrying the weight of the world? What did you discover about abiding in Christ that helps you with this, or can help someone you know?

6. What did you learn about how to love difficult people? How can you apply this to your situation?

   Read Luke 6:22-23. What does Jesus ultimately promise you? How will this influence your outlook?

7. What is the connection in John 15:9-11 between obeying the Lord, abiding in Him, and experiencing joy?

   What is God telling you to do that you are not doing, or what is He telling you to stop doing and you are still doing it? What are you going to do?

8. How does unforgiveness block fruit from growing? Who has hurt you? Have you forgiven this person? What does Ephesians 4:32 say about forgiving people?

9. What effect does abiding in Christ have on your personality? How do you think you can practically express the joy of the Lord to others through your unique personality?

6

THE JOY OF A SATISFIED SOUL

I have a desk in the bedroom where I do my writing. The desk fits into an alcove that has two windows in it. As I sit at the computer with the windows open and smell the fresh summer air, hear the birds singing, and see the sunshine bathing our yard with golden light, I'm filled with great pleasure as I admire the loveliness of God's handiwork.

While most of us have no difficulty enjoying what God has created, some of us have a hard time enjoying the Creator Himself. We can't see God with our eyes or feel Him with our hands. God may, at times, seem abstract and removed. How do you and I find real enjoyment and satisfaction in God? In this chapter, we will discover how to find our deepest joy and satisfaction in God.

DAVID'S SOURCE OF JOY

When I was talking with a woman one time, I casually mentioned something about enjoying God. She looked at me quizzically and said, "I don't think God is enjoyable. I think He is serious."

God *is* serious—in that, He isn't capricious, whimsical, or comical. He is serious about His hatred of sin. He is serious about His love for us. He is serious about fulfilling His Word. But don't we sometimes associate serious with somber? When we do, this may cause us to view God as dull and glum.

In contrast, listen to what David said about God in Psalm 16:8-11:

> I have set the LORD always before me. Because he is at my right hand, I will not be shaken. Therefore my heart is glad and my tongue rejoices; my body also will rest secure, because you will not abandon me to the grave, nor will you let your Holy One see decay. You have made known to me the path of life; you will fill me with joy in your presence, with eternal pleasures at your right hand.

DAVID'S SOURCE OF PLEASURE

Why was David's heart glad? How was he able to rejoice and rest securely? Why was he filled with joy? Were David's circumstances perfect? No.

One key sentence reveals to us the reason for David's joy and contentment: "I have set the LORD always before me" (v. 8).

The Lord was at David's right hand. In the Bible, the right hand signifies the place of favor or prominence. David set the Lord before him as the focus, priority, and supreme love of his life. David didn't set the Lord alongside him—as though He were one of many things in his life. By setting the Lord before him, we see David's desire to glorify God in every aspect of his whole life.

OUR DESIRE FOR PLEASURE

David said, "You have made known to me the path of life; you will fill me with joy in your presence, with eternal pleasures at your right hand" (v. 11). David set the Lord before him and looked to Him as the source of his joy and satisfaction. David expressed His confidence that the Lord could fill him with everlasting pleasure.

As people who are made in the image of God, we have the capacity and desire for pleasure. This is God's good gift to us, and we can thank Him for it. God has given us the ability to experience pleasure from relationships, our job, ministry, a day at the park, a ride in the country, and many other things. God gave us the capacity for enjoyment so we could experience the pleasure of His many good gifts.

But God also gave us the ability to experience pleasure for a deeper reason. God made us with the capacity for pleasure so we, like David, would glorify Him by finding our deepest pleasure and satisfaction in Him. God is a God of everlasting pleasures who desires our pleasure to reach its peak in Him.

Because we live in a world where people selfishly pursue sinful pleasure, we might have the impression that the desire for pleasure is wrong. Joseph Stowell explains pleasure in his book, *Perilous Pursuits*, by saying,

> The pleasure that is a by-product of living to please God is not simply a package of thrills. It is rather, according to the Hebrew of Psalm 1:1, the pleasure of a life that is "straight" or "correct." Not straight in the sense of strict or stoic, but clean, without pretense or hypocrisy, free from the clutter of shame, loss, and regret. Satan appeals to our pleasure instinct with momentary "highs"

> that is fraught with devastating downsides. True pleasure is experienced in the deep, settled rightness of a life committed to God's glory and gain.[1]

If God didn't make us with the capacity for pleasure, we couldn't enjoy an intimate relationship with Him. Our desire for pleasure is not wrong. Where we get off track is when we set other things before us, instead of the Lord, and look to these things to bring us ultimate satisfaction and pleasure.

We may go to church and sing songs about finding our satisfaction in the Lord, but our daily lives may sing a different tune. If we take an honest look at our lives, how many of us would admit to depending on our family, home, job, friends, money, ministry, position, or possessions for our deepest satisfaction?

As good and enjoyable as these gifts are, God never intended them to have the right hand place of prominence in our lives. God has blessed us with temporal gifts to temporarily enjoy, but they cannot give us everlasting joy. An awareness of this distinction is key to enjoying the Lord and having a satisfied soul.

IS JESUS A PART OF YOUR LIFE?

One day when I was reading the newspaper, I saw an article about a religious leader in Chicago who decided to spread the message, door-to-door, that God wants to be a part of our lives. Later on when I discussed the article with my husband, I said, "I wonder what part of a person's life this man thinks God wants. Sixty percent? An hour on Sunday?"

Our families, work, home, and so on are all a part of our lives. But the immense, infinite God of the universe does not fit into our lives like another activity. Nowhere does the Bible say God wants to be a part of our lives.

He wants all of our lives. Nothing less (Gal. 2:20; Rom. 12:1; Mark 8:35).

At first when we hear someone say that God wants to be a part of our lives, we might agree. But when we think it through, we may reach a different conclusion.

Did Jesus give His life on the cross for us, so we would give Him a *part* of our lives? He held nothing back from us. What are we holding back from Him?

When we give God a part of our lives, we mentally put Him on the same level as other things. The infinite, omnipotent God is Lord of the universe, and He must be Lord of our lives.

The idea that God wants to be a part of our lives runs contrary to Scripture because it exalts man and belittles God. This view is born out of a small, inadequate view of God. When we have a small view of God, we give Him a part of our lives—but not our whole lives. When we have an inadequate view of God, we think He is inadequate to fulfill us.

Consequently, we trust in other things for our ultimate satisfaction. We don't set the Lord before us as David did, but we keep Him tucked away in our back pocket.

WHAT ARE YOU SETTING BEFORE YOU?

How we often look for our *life* in people and things, and make God a *part* of our lives. We set other things before us and depend on them to satisfy us, instead of setting the Lord before us and depending on Him for our deepest satisfaction and joy.

For example, the Bible says children are a gift from the Lord (Ps. 127:3). God gives us children as good gifts to enjoy. As our children start to grow up, we realize they won't always be with us. This can be hard for us. It was for me.

For some reason, I always envisioned myself as the mother of babies and preschoolers. When our daughter, Whitney, waved good-bye and stepped onto the school bus at the age of five, I realized my days as the mother of babies and preschoolers had abruptly ended. I wished I could freeze my children so they would always stay little. I wrote in my journal:

> God is showing me that I am clinging to my children. As they move further away, I want to hold on all the more. But as I cling to them I have no freedom, because I know I can't hold onto them forever. God wants me to cling to Him. To cling to God is to follow Him fully (Num. 32:12; Deut. 1:36). Psalm 63:8 says, "My soul clings to you; your right hand upholds me." *Cling* means "to hold together; to adhere as if glued firmly; to hold on tightly or tenaciously; to have a strong emotional attachment or dependency." God wants me glued to Him, not my children.

Jesus asked Peter what was most important to him. Jesus said, "Simon son of John, do you truly love me more than these?" (John 21:15). I feel like Jesus is asking me, "Do you truly love me more than Aaron and Whitney?" Abraham loved Isaac, but he loved God supremely. Hannah loved Samuel, but she loved God supremely.

I remember when Aaron was about five years old, as I was sitting with him on his bed, he said to me, "Mommy, I love you so much." As I went to hug him, he said, "But I love God more." This was what I had been praying for since before he was born! God wants me to say, "I love my children so much, but Lord, I love You more." In this, I experience the freedom to enjoy my kids and enjoy my Lord.

I think of the hymn *When I Survey the Wondrous Cross*. It says, "Love so amazing so divine, demands my soul,

> my life, my all."[2] His love demands nothing less than "My utmost for His highest. I am determined to be absolutely and entirely for Him and Him alone."[3]
>
> Jesus said, "Anyone who loves his father or mother more than me is not worthy of me; anyone who loves his son or daughter more than me is not worthy of me; and anyone who does not take his cross and follow me [cling to Him] is not worthy of me" (Matt. 10:37). Oh, Jesus, I confess my supreme love for You.

If someone had asked me before I wrote that entry in my journal if I loved the Lord supremely, I would have said, "Yes." I didn't realize I had inadvertently set my children before me. But when I consciously set the Lord before me and reaffirmed my supreme love for Him, I enjoyed my relationship with God and my children much more.

Have you inadvertently put someone or something in God's supreme place? Are you are trying to receive everlasting pleasure from temporal gifts?

Deep inside us, you and I have a longing, or hunger, for satisfaction that goes beyond what any person or thing can give. God is the only One who can satisfy the deep hunger of our souls. God, in His kindness, designed us this way to initially draw us to Him and keep us dependent on Him.

OUR ETERNAL SOURCE OF JOY

We know we can't hold onto people and things forever, yet we cling to them. This tension becomes a barrier that prevents us from relaxing and enjoying God's gifts and enjoying God Himself. No person or thing can truly satisfy our souls and give us the deep joy that is found in the Lord.

People disappoint us, the roof leaks, our stocks fall, the car stalls. This is part of life.

That's it! This is *part* of life, but this is not our *life*.

Our life is not found in people and things. Our life is Christ. "When *Christ, who is your life,* appears, then you also will appear with him in glory" (Col. 3:4 emphasis added). David said, "*You* have made known to me the path of *life*; *you will fill me with joy* in your presence, with eternal pleasures at your right hand" (Ps. 16:11 emphasis added).

God never intended us to find everlasting pleasures in temporal enjoyments. Everlasting pleasures are found in the everlasting God. He is our eternal source of joy. David understood this important distinction. He didn't include God on a list of things he had set before him to satisfy his soul. David set the Lord before him and looked to Him for ultimate satisfaction and joy.

Examine your life for things that are blocking your enjoyment of God. What is preventing you from saying, "I have set the LORD always before me"? Is Jesus a part of your life, or is He your life?

BROKEN CISTERNS

Unlike David, the Israelites did not set the Lord before them. Because of their small, inadequate view of God, they sought to satisfy themselves with other things—in their case, pagan idols. In the second chapter of Jeremiah, God lamented over his people saying, "My people have committed two sins: They have forsaken me, the spring of living water, and have dug their own cisterns, broken cisterns that cannot hold water" (v. 13).

Commenting on Jeremiah 2:13, Bible scholars tell us:

> The most reliable and refreshing sources of water in Israel were her natural springs. The water was dependable; and its clear, cool consistency was satisfying. In contrast, the most unreliable source of water was cisterns. Cisterns were large pits dug into the rock and

> covered with plaster. These pits were used to gather rainwater. This water was brackish; and if the rains were below normal, it could run out. Worse yet, if a cistern developed a crack it would not hold the water. To turn from a dependable, pure stream of running water to a broken, brackish cistern was idiotic.[4]

Since the Israelites did not believe the Lord was able to fulfill them, they sought their pleasure elsewhere. God compared their actions to seeking water from broken cisterns. Since broken cisterns served no purpose, why would the Israelites turn from the Lord—the spring of living water—and seek fulfillment from empty, stale holes in the ground?

For the same reason we look for water in empty pits. We cling to the sinful belief that someone or something other than the Lord Jesus can satisfy the thirst of our souls. We need to remember that God calls this sin (Jer. 2:13). It is sin because we don't believe what the Lord tells us about Himself. "For he satisfies the thirsty and fills the hungry with good things" (Ps. 107:9). What it comes down to is this: do we believe in the adequacy of Jesus or don't we? Do we believe He can satisfy us or not?

When our son was doing some off-campus exploring his freshman year in college, a man approached him and said, "I'm not asking you for any money, but could you please give me some food? I haven't eaten anything since yesterday, and I'm so hungry." Aaron felt compassion for the man, so he took him to a restaurant and bought him a meal.

Suppose Aaron had taken this man to a furniture store and bought him a new chair. Or to a health club and bought him a membership. Or given him a free pass to an amusement park. Would any of these things have satisfied the man's hunger?

What does a hungry, thirsty person need? Food and drink. No

person, possession, investment, amusement, or accomplishment can satisfy a hungry, thirsty soul. It makes as much sense to try to stuff these into our stomachs as into our souls! No amount of things can satisfy souls that were created by God and for God.

If we depend on dry, empty wells to quench our thirst, how will we feel? Dry and empty. All of our efforts to draw water from empty wells are nothing but a vain attempt to quench our thirst from a stale hole in the ground. If we try to fill the thirst of our souls for satisfaction and joy with something other than the Lord, we feel *dis*satisfied and lack joy. When we have a small, inadequate view of God, we occupy ourselves with small things that are inadequate to fill our souls with the joy we long for.

ENDLESS, REFRESHING WATER

Compare the futile attempt of trying to draw water from dry wells to the refreshing words of Jesus:

> Everyone who drinks this water will be thirsty again, but whoever drinks the water I give him will never thirst. Indeed, the water I give him will become in him a spring of water welling up to eternal life (John 4:13-14).

> I am the bread of life. He who comes to me will never go hungry, and he who believes in me will never be thirsty (John 6:35).

> If anyone is thirsty, let him come to me and drink. Whoever believes in me, as the Scripture has said, streams of living water will flow from within him (John 7:37-38).

When Jesus spoke those words, bread was a staple of life. If a person didn't have bread, the person didn't live. And, of course, no one can live without water. Jesus directly compared Himself to water and bread to say that He is spiritual life. As food and water give life to the body and satisfy the stomach, Jesus gives us spiritual life and satisfies our souls. If we want joy-filled lives, then our lives must be filled with Jesus. Are you and I setting the Lord before us and trusting Him to fill us with the joy of a satisfied soul?

NO FOOD IN THE SNOW

One afternoon my husband and I drove to a historic town and browsed through the shops. In one of the shops a picture called *Shortening Winter's Day* caught my attention. When Dean saw how much I liked the picture, he told me to buy it. I appreciated him telling me to buy it, but I decided not to get it because I thought it was too expensive. Although I didn't buy the picture that day, I eventually bought it elsewhere (for much less!) and hung it in our dining room.

I was initially drawn to the picture because I like sheep. But after I looked at it for a while, I noticed something strange about the sheep. As you read the description of the picture, think about where you are looking for your satisfaction and joy.

The setting sun casts orange rays of light onto the glistening snow. In the twilight hours, a shepherd stands before his flock of sheep with a bundle of hay on his back. Strangely, most of the sheep seem unaware of the shepherd's presence. Some sheep stand with their backs to him. Their noses are buried in the snow—as though they expect to find food there.

Some of the other sheep are facing the shepherd, but their eyes aren't on him. They are watching the rest of the sheep and seem to be depending on them for their food.

A third, smaller group of sheep is gathered at the feet of the shepherd. Their heads are pointed up toward him; their eyes look expectantly into his face; their mouths are open wide.

What group of sheep do you identify with? Are you depending on the Shepherd to satisfy your hunger, or are you looking elsewhere?

DEVELOPING AN APPETITE FOR THE LORD

Although the shepherd was the only one who could feed the sheep, most of them were looking elsewhere for their food. Jesus is the only One who can feed our souls and satisfy us with true joy. The psalmist said, "As the deer pants for streams of water, so my soul pants for you, O God. My soul thirsts for God, for the living God" (42:1-2).

Do you and I share the psalmist's deep longing for God? Do our souls pant for Him? Maybe it's difficult for us to relate to the psalmist's intense desire. We want to have such a desire for God, but we don't. How can we develop a hunger and thirst for God and enjoy greater intimacy with Him? The following suggestions may help:

- Confess your lack of intense desire to the Lord. He knows what you're thinking anyway. This gets it out in the open.

- Ask God to place a deep hunger and thirst for Him within you. When I realize I'm not longing for the Lord as I would like to, I pray that I would desire Him with the desire He has for me. "I will put a desire in their hearts to worship me" (Jer. 32:40 NLT).

- Examine your life to see if you're setting the Lord before you or something else. Ask God to show you the barriers that are hindering you from enjoying intimacy with Him.

> "Search me, O God, and know my heart; test me and know my anxious thoughts. See if there is any offensive way in me, and lead me in the way everlasting" (Ps. 139:23-24).

- Take purposeful steps to move toward the Lord by spending time with Him in prayer and in His Word. "When you said, 'Seek My face,' my heart said to You, 'Your face, LORD, I will seek' " (Ps. 27:8 NKJV).

DAVID'S THIRST FOR GOD

As we turn our attention to Psalm 63:1-5, we will continue to learn how to develop a greater appetite for God as we see David's longing for God, his confidence that God could satisfy his longing, and David's joy of experiencing a satisfied soul.

> O God, you are my God, earnestly I seek you; my soul thirsts for you, my body longs for you, in a dry and weary land where there is no water. I have seen you in the sanctuary and beheld your power and your glory. Because your love is better than life, my lips will glorify you. I will praise you as long as I live, and in your name I will lift up my hands. My soul will be satisfied as with the richest of foods; with singing lips my mouth will praise you.

When David wrote this Psalm, he was in the wilderness of Judea fleeing for his life. Imagine how David felt knowing that the man who was chasing him was his own son, Absalom! Although David was the king of Israel, he was running from his son like a fugitive.

If you and I were in David's situation, what might our thoughts be? As we breathlessly hid among the rocks and in caves, would we cry out a desperate prayer of "Help"? Would we feverishly try to figure out the best way to elude Absalom? Would we wonder if God still loved us? Would we be overcome with fear and anger?

Martyn Lloyd-Jones explains what was foremost on David's mind as he hid in the wilderness:

> It is David's greatest desire to feel the presence of God; to know that He is with him and that He is looking down upon him. Because David—and this is the wonderful thing—was even more concerned about this than he was about his circumstances. He is in a dry and thirsty land without water; he is surrounded by enemies; he knows that some very able men are conspiring with Absalom to bring about not only his defeat but probably his death also, in order that Absalom may become king. His situation could not be more precarious. But in spite of all this, his biggest concern is not with the circumstances, though, naturally, he is concerned about them. No, the real desire of David's heart, and he puts it therefore in this expressive language, is: "My soul thirsteth for thee, my flesh..." The whole man is involved; there is nothing about him that is not, in this way, longing and thirsting for the presence of God.[5]

David wasn't filled with anger or fear, and He didn't doubt God's love. Instead, David's heart erupted with praise to God. David's son wanted him dead, yet David was filled with joy! How was this possible?

We find the explanation to David's joy in his view of God. David did not have a small, inadequate view of God that made Him a part of his life. David had an exalted view of God. "O God, *you* are my God" (Ps. 63:1 emphasis added).

An exalted view of God is essential to enjoying Him. Because David had the right view of God, he depended on the Lord to satisfy Him—not his circumstances. In the midst of the wilderness, pursued by his enemies, David sought to know the joy of the Lord's intimate presence.

Do you feel like you are in a wilderness? Do tensions, uncertainty, and fear pursue you like Absalom pursued David? In Psalm 27:1, David wrote: "The LORD is my light and my salvation—whom shall I fear? The LORD is the stronghold of my life—of whom shall I be afraid?" David placed all of his hope in what he saw in God, not in what he saw around him.

Although Absalom was intent on pursuing his father, David was intent on pursuing his heavenly Father. "*Earnestly* I seek *you*; my soul thirsts for *you*, my body longs for *you*, in a dry and weary land where there is no water" (Ps. 63:1 emphasis added). David's physical thirst is a picture of his spiritual thirst for God. The dry wilderness intensified David's desire to intentionally seek the Lord—the One in whom he placed his hope.

INTENT ON SEEKING GOD

How intentional are you and I in our desire to seek the Lord? Do we run to Him only in times of trouble, or are we walking with Him day-by-day? David didn't turn to the Lord only when life became difficult; he had a consistent walk with the Him each day. When trials invaded David's life, he continued his habit of earnestly seeking the Lord.

I have a friend who decided to rearrange her schedule so she could spend one afternoon a week to especially focus on the Lord. When she shared her plan with another Christian, this person advised her to not overdo it and to try once a month instead.

My friend said, "I realize at the end of the afternoon I won't have anything tangible to show for my time spent with God, so it may seem like I'm unproductive. Maybe spending a prolonged period of time with the Lord might look like a waste, but I'd like to try my original plan."

The fast pace at which many of us live makes us especially conscious of not wasting our time. As we try to squeeze as much as we can into our busy days, we've become adept at doing several things at once. I've seen people reading books while driving their cars. (Not something I'd recommend!) We talk on our cell phones while we run errands. We pray and listen to music while we fast walk. We read our Bible while we're on the treadmill.

But are we only praying while we're walking and only reading our Bible when we're on the treadmill? Do we sandwich these things together because we don't want to "waste time" with Jesus when we could be doing something "productive" at the same time? Do you and I take time to be with the Lord, to ponder Him, and to reflect on His Word? Are we trying to squeeze Jesus into our lives like a granola bar, or are we enjoying a feast with Him? Can we, like David, say, "Earnestly I seek you"? (Ps. 63:1).

In the Psalms, we read: "Be still, and know that I am God" (46:10). For some of us, being still may be the hardest thing we do this week! Are we willing to step off the treadmill, catch our breath, and say to the Lord, "Speak, for your servant is listening"? (1 Samuel 3:10). How will we intentionally seek Jesus and show Him we value Him above all else?

Martha and Mary

In Luke 10, we see two women who were intentional, but not in the same pursuit. Martha was intent on making Jesus dinner—so intent that she lost her perspective on what was most important. Martha viewed her work as productive, but she thought Mary could make better use of her time than to singularly focus on Jesus. Martha came to Jesus and said,

> "Lord, don't you care that my sister has left me to do the work by myself? Tell her to help me!"
> "Martha, Martha," the Lord answered, "you are worried and upset about so many things, but only one thing is needed. Mary has chosen what is better, and it will not be taken away from her" (vs. 41-42).

While Martha was busy running around the kitchen, imagine the rich spiritual food Mary was receiving from Jesus. Mary enjoyed a feast because she was willing to "waste time" with Jesus by focusing on Him alone. Martha was left hungry, frustrated, and angry. How can you reorganize your day so you can earnestly seek the Lord and enjoy a banquet with Him?

CONTENTMENT IN A DIFFICULT PLACE

As we continue in Psalm 63, we see David's desire to joyfully worship God. "I have seen you in the sanctuary and beheld your power and your glory" (v. 2). Although David longed to worship the Lord in Jerusalem, the Judean wilderness became David's place of worship as He exalted the Lord where he was. David found himself in a difficult place, but he turned it into a place of worship and praise.

Are you in a difficult place? Maybe you are facing surgery...your marriage is not what you hoped it would be...you suffer from chronic pain...you have lost a loved one...you have lost your job...the future seems uncertain.

One thing *is* certain about life: it is full of difficult places. When I think of a person in the Bible who repeatedly found himself in difficult places, I think of the Apostle Paul. Yet listen to what Paul said while he was a prisoner, chained to a guard: "I know what it is to be in need, and I know what it is to have plenty. I have learned the secret of being content in any and every situation, whether well fed or hungry, whether living in plenty or in want. I can do everything through him who gives me strength" (Phil. 4:12-13).

Paul was a prisoner *in* a difficult place, but he was not a prisoner *of* his difficult place. Paul did not let his prison determine his attitude or diminish his joy. He refused to allow the prison to conform his thinking to its condition. Instead, he transformed his prison into a place of contentment and joy because he did not let his circumstances determine who he was. Like David, Paul turned his place of adversity into a place of praise because he found his joy in the Lord, instead of his circumstances.

I have a greeting card on my kitchen counter that says, "If you don't like something, change it. If you can't change it, change the way you think about it!" The front of the card shows a girl painting a landscape of trees and brightly colored flowers on the walls of a room. The room she is painting has a window, but the view out the window is a brick wall.

When I look at the card, I'm reminded of my friend, Louise. While she was at a conference, she fell and broke her ankle. When I talked with Louise after she came home from the hospital, the first thing that came out of her mouth was praise to God for all the ways He took care of her in the accident. She also said that being laid up would give her an opportunity to catch up on telephone calls and encourage people.

Louise turned her place of adversity into a place of worship and praise. She painted a beautiful landscape when all she could look at were walls. How can you turn your difficult place into a place of contentment and praise?

DAVID'S LOVE FOR GOD

In Psalm 63:3, David continued his joyful praise to God. "Because your love is better than life, my lips will glorify you. I will praise you as long as I live, and in your name I will lift up my hands." David declared that knowing the love of the Lord meant more to him than whether he lived or died. This was no glib statement on the part of David. The threat of being murdered at the hands of his son loomed before David as a real possibility.

Yet David could honestly say the Lord's love was better than life because the Lord was not a part of David's life. The Lord was his life. David set the Lord before everything—even his own life. David viewed his physical life as inconsequential when compared to the spiritual life and love he received from the Lord.

Many years later, the Apostle Paul, who was also hunted by his enemies, wrote in the same vein: "But I do not consider my life of any account as dear to myself, in order that I may finish my course, and the ministry which I received from the Lord Jesus, to testify solemnly of the gospel of the grace of God" (Acts 20:24 NASB).

Both Paul and David saw themselves as dispensable for the kingdom of God. The Lord could do with them as He pleased, and whatever He did with them would be good and right.

Do you and I have this same view of our lives? Do we say, "Lord, whatever You do with me is good and right, so do whatever"? We hold onto ourselves tightly, don't we? We tell God, "You know I don't want ___________, and please don't ever ask me to _______________." (Fill in the blanks.)

One day as I was praying, I realized my prayer sounded like me telling God about all the things I didn't need in my life. When I actually listened to myself and heard what I was saying, I realized my prayer was no prayer at all. Then I prayed, "Lord, I'm taking my hands off my life. I don't know what I need. All I know is I need You. You do with me as You will. You have free reign in my life."

Are you willing to take your hands off your life and say to the Lord, "Whatever You do with me, Lord, is good and right, so do whatever"? It may seem scary, but this is faith. Imagine the incredible joy that awaits those who dare to abandon themselves to God! "But as for me, I shall sing of Thy strength; Yes, I shall joyfully sing of Thy lovingkindness in the morning, For Thou hast been my stronghold, And a refuge in the day of my distress" (Ps. 59:16 NASB).

NO TURNING BACK

When David faced the threat of death, he affirmed to the Lord that he would not die turning away from Him. No matter how long David lived—whether a few more hours or many years—he determined to exalt the Lord by praising Him with his last breath. "I will praise you as long as I live, and in your name I will lift up my hands" (Ps. 63:4). In a posture of having his hands raised before God, David indicated his complete submission to the Lord.

I received a letter from my friend who is a missionary in a country where Christians are killed. She told me some of the Christians in a certain village were so afraid, they started to revert to sorcery. Tom (name changed), who lives in the village, preached a powerful sermon on following Christ.

In response to his preaching, the people brought their objects of the occult to the church and burned them. Tom said, "We could die from malaria or from a boat sinking or anything. We will all die someday. But we do not want to die turning away from the Lord."

David determined that no matter what happened or how desperate his situation, God would always be his God. Are you in a desperate situation? How important it is to receive our strength and joy from the Lord by praising Him as the sovereign Lord over our lives. "O God, *you* are my God....I *will* praise you as long as I live (63:1,4 emphasis added).

SOUL FOOD

Although David's diet in the wilderness may have consisted of whatever food he could find, he was so caught up in the joy of praising God that he hardly seemed aware of his physical need for food and water. He said, "My soul will be satisfied as with the richest of foods; with singing lips my mouth will praise you" (Ps. 63:5).

David's words remind us of the account in John 4, where Jesus' physical hunger and thirst were preempted by His desire to do the Father's will. Jesus was thirsty and hungry after walking many miles to the town of Sychar, in Samaria. When Jesus came to Jacob's well, He asked a Samaritan woman, who had come to draw water, to give Him a drink. The conversation Jesus began with this woman led to her believing in Jesus as the Messiah. In her hurry to tell others about Jesus, she ran back to town and neglected to give Him the drink of water He had requested (vs. 4-30).

Jesus was still thirsty and hungry when His disciples returned from the town with food. When they came to the well, they urged Him to eat, saying,

> "Rabbi, eat something."
> But he said to them, "I have food to eat that you know nothing about."
> Then his disciples said to each another, "Could someone have brought him food?"
> "My food," said Jesus, "is to do the will of him who sent me and to finish his work" (vs. 31-34).

Jesus' joy of doing the Father's will by saving one Samaritan woman was so deeply satisfying that it eclipsed His physical thirst and hunger. Similarly, David's deep desire for the Lord surpassed every other desire—even his desire for food. Although David was physically hungry, he feasted with satisfied delight in the joy of the Lord's intimate presence. "My soul is satisfied as with marrow and fatness, and my mouth offers praises with joyful lips" (Ps. 63:5 NASB).

As a good meal satisfies the stomach, David's soul was satisfied with the Lord. David's stomach was empty, yet his soul was filled with the richest of gourmet foods. His lips were dry from the desert sun, yet they joyfully glorified the Lord for His great goodness and faithfulness.

As we observe David's response in the wilderness, we see that joy is the spillover of a soul that it filled with God. David said, "You have filled my heart with greater joy than when their grain and new wine abound" (Ps. 4:7).

As the Lord satisfies the thirst of our soul with Himself, our thirst for Him increases. As God fills us with Himself, we long for Him all the more. The more we hunger and thirst for God, the greater our satisfaction in Him. Our level of satisfaction in the Lord is proportionate to our appetite for Him. " 'And my people shall be satisfied with my goodness,' says the LORD" (Jer. 31:14 NKJV).

Jesus said, "Blessed [joyful] are those who hunger and thirst for righteousness, for they will be filled" (Matt. 5:6). As we hunger and thirst for Him, He fills our hearts with the joy of a satisfied soul. We experience the pleasure our souls long for when our souls long for Jesus. Joy is the everlasting pleasure of finding our deepest satisfaction in Jesus Christ.

A.W. Tozer wrote this prayer about the joy of a satisfied soul in his book, *The Pursuit of God.* Let's also make it our prayer:

> O God, I have tasted Thy goodness, and it has both satisfied me and made me thirsty for more. I am painfully conscious of my need of further grace. I am ashamed of my lack of desire. O God, the Triune God, I want to want

Thee; I long to be filled with longing; I thirst to be made more thirsty still. Show me Thy glory, I pray Thee, so that I may know Thee indeed. Begin in mercy a new work of love within me. Say to my soul, 'Rise up, my love, my fair one, and come away.' Then give me grace to rise up and follow Thee up from this misty lowland where I have wandered so long. In Jesus' name. Amen.[6]

Responding to God's Word

1. David said, "I have set the LORD always before me" (Ps. 63:8). How would you describe what this means? How does your view of God affect your joy and satisfaction?

2. What would you say the difference is between Jesus being a part of your life and Him being your life? What do the following verses say about what it means to have Christ as your life?

    Mark 8:34-37

    2 Corinthians 5:15

    Galatians 2:20

    Philippians 1:21

    Colossians 3:3-4

    1 John 4:9

3. What happens to your relationship with God when you rely on temporal things to bring you ultimate satisfaction?

4. Read John 21:15. What are the "these" in your life?

   Are you willing to surrender your "these" to God? You may want to write a prayer to Him regarding this:

   Father,

5. What group of sheep did you identify with? How does Isaiah 55:1-2 relate to the sheep illustration?

6. What did you learn about developing a greater hunger and thirst for the Lord? How will you apply this?

7. How were David and Paul able to experience contentment in their difficult situations? What did you discover from them that encourages you in your difficult situation?

8. Read Psalm 107:9. What do you think the correlation is between your hunger for the Lord and your satisfaction in Him? What does the level of your desire for Him practically reveal about what you are depending on for your ultimate satisfaction and joy?

7

JOY IN THE MIDST OF TRIALS

Karl Marx, the founder of communism, referred to religion as the opiate or drug of the people because he observed that the peasants who focused on God were able to persevere through their difficult circumstances. Marx thought faith was like a sedative that helped people to endure suffering.

For a revolution to succeed, he knew the peasants would need to take their eyes off God and focus on their circumstances. In 1917, Vladimir Lenin, a devotee of Marx, stirred up the Russian peasants and led a violent revolution that toppled the regime of the czars and ushered in the bleak years of communism.

Unlike the Russian peasants who focused on their circumstances and revolted, our joy isn't centered on our circumstances, but in Jesus Christ. As believers, we not only persevere through trials, but our trials become a path of joy.

How can trials possibly be a route of joy? We all know the journey through life is not an easy walk. We encounter many difficult trials along the way.

In this chapter, and the next, we want to paint a realistic picture of how we can know joy in the midst of trials. What does joy look like when our child has an accident, when we're told we have cancer, when a loved one dies, or when the answers to our questions don't come?

Jesus talks to us about joy in the context of life's trials. He speaks about joy in real ways so hurting people can receive real comfort, and those who are distressed might find encouragement, and those who are discouraged would experience hope.

Let Jesus speak to your heart. Hear His words of comfort and hope as we continue on the path of joy. May the Lord deeply encourage and strengthen us as we learn how we can know the reality of joy when our path is filled with rocks and sharp turns.

CONSIDER IT PURE JOY?

We will begin by focusing on James 1:2-4:

> Consider it pure joy, my brothers, whenever you face trials of many kinds, because you know that the testing of your faith develops perseverance. Perseverance must finish its work so that you may be mature and complete, not lacking anything.

James encouraged the Jewish believers who were suffering, to consider it pure joy when they faced many kinds of trials. By telling them to face their trials with joy, he wasn't teaching them to adopt a stoical approach. He didn't tell them to deny the pain of the trial and pretend like it didn't exist. Neither was James making light of their suffering or glossing over their trials.

Although the hand of James wrote these words, they were spoken from the mouth of the Lord. Jesus used the pen of James to encourage the Jewish believers and all of us who would read His Word. The One who tells us to consider it pure joy when we face our many trials, is the One who suffered through the deepest and most painful trials anyone could ever endure.

Jesus left the glory of heaven to live among people who paid Him no honor. His closest friends abandoned Him (Mark 14:50). He was hated, laughed at, and humiliated (15:18-19). His beard was torn off His face to show utter contempt (Is. 50:6). His back was split open from multiple lashings (Mark 15:15). His face was bruised and swollen from brutal punches (15:19). A crown of thorns was pressed into His head (15:17). He was tortured to death by crucifixion (15:37). He was forsaken, for a time, even by His own Father (Matt. 27:46).

When the Lord tells us to consider it pure joy when we face our trials, He personally knows what trials are all about. It's *because* He identifies with us so deeply that He tells us to consider our trials pure joy. Because He has gone through so much pain, suffering, and sorrow and emerged victoriously, He takes our hand and compassionately tells us to also consider it all joy when we encounter our many trials.

James used the word *brothers* to add tenderness to his instruction on joy. We remember that Jesus also referred to those who love Him as "brothers" (Matt. 12:49). As beloved members of His family, the Lord speaks to us about trials as One who understands and deeply cares about every detail of our lives.

He doesn't compare our trials with the trials of other people. Jesus never brushes over our trials as meaningless or insignificant. He doesn't tell us to make lemonade out of our lemons. That kind of platitude might be acceptable if we have a broken fingernail, but what.if we have a broken heart?

Is your heart breaking today? Jesus knows what it's like to be broken. He is our sympathetic Savior who perfectly identifies with us in our pain and brokenness. "For we do not have a high priest who is unable to sympathize with our weaknesses, but we have one who has been tempted in every way, just as we are—yet without sin" (Heb. 4:15).

Several years ago, a man my husband worked with dropped dead of a heart attack while playing golf. Tom and his wife, Jane, had thoroughly enjoyed one another, so it was natural for Jane to continue to speak about her husband after his death. Jane mentioned to me that when she talked about Tom, people often became uneasy and tried to change the subject. Although Jane was the one hurting, she found herself thinking of how she could make others feel more comfortable.

The Lord doesn't change the subject or get uncomfortable when we talk to Him about our trials. He loves us, and He wants us to come to Him and pour out our hearts. He understands what you and I experience as we go through our trials. He can say to us, "I know exactly how you feel."

NOT *IF* BUT *WHEN*

Although we might wish life consisted of all smooth sailing and we could someday breeze into the heavenly port, we know this isn't so. God doesn't tell us when we become a Christian all of our problems vanish and we never suffer. Trials will happen.

The Lord is compassionate and understanding, and He is also straightforward about what to expect from life on earth. He tells us that trials are not a matter of "if" but "when."

"Consider it pure joy, my brothers, *whenever* you face trials of many kinds" (James 1:2 emphasis added). God never says "if" we should happen to go through trials. It's always "when." It's going to happen. Trials are an unavoidable part of our human experience. "Man is born to trouble as surely as sparks fly upward" (Job 5:7).

Because of the inevitability of trials, we shouldn't be surprised when they come upon us. Peter said, "Dear friends, do not be surprised at the painful trial you are suffering, as though something strange were happening to you" (1 Peter 4:12).

In Isaiah 43:1-2, we read about the certainty of trials:

> Fear not, for I have redeemed you; I have summoned you by name; you are mine. *When* you pass through the waters, I will be with you; and when you pass through the rivers, they will not sweep over you. *When* you walk through the fire, you will not be burned; the flames will not set you ablaze (emphasis added).

When we walk through deep waters of adversity, we get wet. *When* we walk through fiery trials, we feel the heat. *When* the waves crash against us and the heat of our trial is painfully intense, what is our hope? Our joy?

Our hope and joy cannot come from what we see around us, but only and always from what we see in Jesus. When we pass through deep waters and walk through the fire, He is with us. In Isaiah 43:1-2, when the Lord is speaking to us about the certainty of deep waters and fire, He comforts our hearts by revealing to us the certainty of His presence. "When you pass through the waters, *I will be with you*" (Is. 43:2 emphasis added).

As you pass through your many trials, you are not alone. Jesus is with you. If He were ever going to leave you, it would have been at the cross. But Jesus was separated from His Father then, so He could say to you now, "Never will I leave you; never will I forsake you" (Heb. 13:5).

His grip on you never loosens. Not for a moment.

God doesn't promise us health and wealth, but He does promise us Himself. When the waves are swirling around us and we don't think we can stand one more minute of heat, the Lord stands beside us to strengthen us with His presence and His promises. Joy is founded on the unfailing presence and promises of God:

- *He has redeemed us and called us by name.* "See, I have engraved you on the palms of my hands" (Is. 49:16). His intimate knowledge of us and all we are going through gives us **calmness**.
- *We belong to Him.* "You are precious and honored in my sight, and...I love you" (Is. 43:4). Knowing we are His precious possession gives us **comfort**.
- *He is always with us.* "I will not forget you!" (Is. 49:15). The nearness of His presence gives us **companionship**.

As you and I face our trials, it helps to remember that the events in our lives are not the result of random happenstance. No trial enters our lives apart from the sovereign hand of God. When things seem out-of-control, God is still in control. Our trials must first pass through the hands of our loving Father before they can touch us.

CONSIDER IT PURE JOY

Our son unexpectedly came home from college one weekend to seek our counsel about a trial he was going through. My heart went out to Aaron as my husband and I talked and prayed with him. As I walked into the den before he went back to school, I saw Aaron staring out the window. I sat down next to him on the couch and said, "We don't learn deep lessons in shallow water."

Like a tidal wave, trials sweep across us unpredictably. They don't give us advance notice before they enter our lives. Our trials don't knock before they come in. They come upon us when we least expect them, and we don't know how long they will stay.

This is why we need to consider how we are going to face our trials, so we'll be prepared when they come. James said, "*Consider* it pure joy, my brothers, whenever you face trials of many kinds" (1:2 emphasis added). We are to consider, or once and for all decide, how we will respond to our trials. Although none of us know when to expect our next trial or what it might be, we can choose right now how we will respond to it.

We prepare for our trials by reminding ourselves to have a joyful response of trust in the Lord as we remember that He has redeemed us and called us by name. We belong to Him. He is with us.

TRIALS PRODUCE PERSEVERANCE

James said, "Consider it pure joy, my brothers, whenever you face trials of many kinds, because *you know* that the testing of your faith develops perseverance. Perseverance must finish its work so that you may be mature and complete, not lacking anything" (1:2-4 emphasis added).

We are to face our trials with joy because of what we know. What do we know about the trial? What purpose does it serve?

A trial is a testing of our faith that produces perseverance or endurance. This testing or trying refers to a refining process. As a goldsmith heats up gold to refine it, the impurities or dross rise to the surface and are skimmed away. After the gold cools down, what is left is strong, pure gold that has passed the test of endurance. The gold is proven to be genuine because it has passed the testing process.

Our faith is a precious commodity to God. It is more valuable than all the gold on earth. In God's loving hands, our trials become His tools to strengthen our faith and show it is genuine. God uses trials as a refining process to carefully strip out the impurities in our lives and make us more like Jesus. This is how our faith is perfected or matured.

The wood floors in two rooms in my home illustrate this refining process. Before my husband and I bought the wood, the boards were scrubbed with a wire brush to remove the soft part of the wood. Once the soft grain was removed, what remained was the strongest, most durable wood.

Many times our trials feel like we're being scrubbed with a wire brush, and in a sense we are. Our trials are like a wire brush that God uses to scrub out our reliance upon ourselves and show us how much we must depend on Him. As we depend less on ourselves and more on God, our faith is strengthened. As much as the scrubbing hurts, without the wire brush our faith would be soft and weak.

Trials reveal to us our weak spots and thrust us into greater dependency upon the Lord. Each time the wire brush of a trial passes across us, our faith is strengthened and refined as our weak, self-reliance falls away. What remains is strong, durable faith.

As we persevere through trials, our faith develops a wholeness or completeness and lacks nothing because the weak spots are worked out. Our faith, like gold, is approved as pure and genuine. James said, "Blessed [joyful] is the man who perseveres under trial; for once he has been approved, he will receive the crown of life, which the Lord has promised to those who love Him" (1:12 NASB).

HE IS FAITHFUL

One morning I shared the illustration of the wood floor with my friend, Marcia, whose son, Matthew, had recently broken his leg in four places in a skateboard accident. Marcia responded to hearing about the scrubbing process by saying, "God is so good. If it weren't for trials, I don't think we would trust Him as much. During these trying times we learn to depend on God the most and experience our greatest intimacy with Him."

As Matthew lay in bed recovering from surgery, Marcia, and her husband, Larry, were concerned that the growth of Matthew's leg might possibly be stunted because the breaks were near a growth plate. When Marcia called the high school to report what had happened to her son, the school secretary exclaimed, "Your son will never be the same again! He won't ever do the things he used to do!"

Marcia told me, "I didn't let her words make me feel afraid. We have been through many trials, and each time we have seen God's faithfulness to us. This trial will be no different."

God had faithfully brought Marcia and Larry through their past trials, and He would once again be faithful to bring them through their latest trial. They would emerge from this trial as they had from all the others—with a stronger, more resilient faith, joyfully praising God for His faithfulness to them.

Like Marcia and Larry, you and I have the courage to persevere through our trials with joy because we know the testing process will produce a faith that gleams and endures like fine gold. The Apostle Paul said, "We also rejoice in our sufferings, because *we know* that suffering produces perseverance" (Rom. 5:3 emphasis added). Trials prove the genuine beauty of our faith as we persevere through the trial.

REJOICE IN THE LORD

Listen to these comforting words Peter wrote to those who were enduring severe trials:

> In this you greatly rejoice, though now for a little while you may have had to suffer grief in all kinds of trials. These have come so that your faith—of greater worth than gold, which perishes even though refined by fire—may be proved genuine and may result in praise, glory and honor when Jesus Christ is revealed. Though you have not seen him, you love him; and even though you do not see him now, you believe in him and are filled with an inexpressible and glorious joy, for you are receiving the goal of your faith, the salvation of your souls (1 Peter 1:6-9).

Both Peter and James referred to all kinds of trials, and both men also talked about joy in association with trials. Neither of them, however, said to rejoice in the trial itself. Peter clearly said the believers were suffering grief in their trials. God is not demanding us to be ironclad masochists who consider the grief of a trial pure joy. James didn't say to consider our *trials* pure joy. He said to consider it pure joy whenever we *face* trials. Our joy isn't in the trial, but in the Lord.

For instance, Marcia didn't rejoice over her son's injury. Her joy was in the Lord and His faithfulness to them. While imprisoned, Paul wrote: "Rejoice *in the Lord always*, I will say it again; rejoice!" (Phil. 4:4 emphasis added). Paul didn't rejoice because he was locked up in a filthy prison; he rejoiced in the Lord.

Our circumstances change, but the Lord never does. He is, therefore, always worthy of our praise and rejoicing. Joy isn't found in our changing circumstances, but in our faithful Lord who never changes. "*In him our hearts rejoice*, for we trust in his holy name" (Ps. 33:21 emphasis added).

Like James, Peter saw trials as a means of rejoicing because of what they produce. Although gold is able to withstand a refining through fire, it is of temporal value. Our faith—that is refined through the fire of trials—is shown to be eternally valuable. The result of our enduring the refining process is the proof that our faith is real.

As genuine believers, we will someday give praise, glory, and honor to the Lord in person. Although we don't see Him now, we love Him and trust in Him. We rejoice *in Him* as we go through our trials.

As Marcia will attest, when we go through our trials praising God, we experience a deep oneness with Him. Peter referred to this intimate communion with the Lord as "an inexpressible and glorious joy" (1 Peter 1:8). It's a joy without earthly explanation. It's a heavenly joy that leaves us humbled and speechless before our awesome God.

A JOURNEY TO JOY

I appreciate a friend of mine giving me a personal excerpt from her journal. In her journal, she describes her path to discovering joy and peace in the midst of a deep, painful trial. Her words remind me of what Peter said about an inexpressible and glorious joy. This is what she said:

> When faced with the diagnosis of breast cancer, I remember feeling so sad and upset with God that I may have to face the possibility of not being able to see my boys grow into adulthood. I was so saddened and depressed because suddenly the story God was writing for me was completely different from the story I had written for myself.

My story had me growing old with my husband and seeing what kind of adults my boys turned out to be—including seeing their choice of jobs and wives. I even had some eventual grandchild scripts and retirement days with my husband scripts—well written and preserved for editing and improvement as time passed.

I was suddenly faced with the reality that my life may not coincide with the stories I had written. I didn't realize I had written them until the discouragement came up with the discrepancy! I discovered I had written the stories when I was searching my soul to find out why I was so frightened and sad.

I remember thinking, *If I have to face an early death and not see my boys grow up, if I have to watch the boys and my husband watch me die, how could I ever feel happy again?* How could I be at peace with that? I hated that story. Mine was much better!

It was during this time that I sensed God asking me if I would receive His joy and peace despite my circumstances. He seemed to say, "Did you think My promise for joy and peace was only if your circumstances fit your plan? Do you think I'm too small to give you joy and peace even in this? Are you willing to receive joy and peace from Me, even if I remove you from your family?"

Ouch! I had to think long and hard on that one. If I could not experience joy and peace, is it because I'm too stubborn? Is it because I'm too mad at God for altering my plan—my perfect, long life script? I realized that cooperating with God and accepting His script was a necessary step to receiving His joy and peace.

God offers us joy and peace that passes all human understanding. It's always available to us, but we often settle for so much less. We can rest on the faithfulness of God, despite our circumstances. As we embrace His script and consent to put His kingdom first—even in the darkest circumstances—He will fill us up with Himself and fill our hearts with a joy and peace that are impossible to explain.

This does not mean I have to feel "happy" about losing my family. It means God can fill me immeasurably to ease the sorrow of lost hopes and dreams. Will I allow Him to do that in all areas of my life? "You have filled my heart with greater joy than when their grain and new wine abound" (Ps. 4:7).

GOD'S FAITHFULNESS TO US

My friend said, "We can rest on the faithfulness of God, despite our circumstances." As you and I face our many trials, we may worry whether our faith will hold up. When we go through a trial, we don't trust in *our* faith to sustain us, but in the faithfulness of *God* to sustain us. The faith that is tested in the trial is our faith in God's faithfulness to us.

His faithfulness will not fail, and on that we can stake our faith. He has redeemed us and called us by name. We belong to Him. He is always with us. Our joy is rooted in God's faithfulness. "God is faithful, through whom you were called into fellowship with His Son, Jesus Christ our Lord" (1 Cor. 1:9 NASB).

Trials don't create faith where none exists. Faith is not created in the crisis. Rather, the crisis proves the quality and authenticity of the faith that is already there. Trials purify and strengthen existing faith.

As we are tested through trials, we see again and again God's faithfulness to us. We remember how God was faithful to bring us through our last trial, and we believe He will be faithful to bring us through our present trial. This builds greater confidence or faith in God, as we trust less in ourselves and more in Him.

This is how the refining process of trials works to make our faith strong and durable. As we see how God continually gives us His strength to persevere through our trials, we have hope and joy to persevere through future trials. We consider it pure joy when we encounter various trials because we know, by experience, that the testing of our faith is the process God uses to mature us. Our joy is in God, who is faithful to complete His work of strengthening our faith.

In Colossians, we read these encouraging words: "Being strengthened with all power according to his glorious might so that you may have great endurance and patience, and joyfully giving thanks to the Father" (1:11,12). Our perseverance through the trial proves the genuineness of our faith. And because our faith *is* genuine, God gives us the strength and power to endure and joyfully give thanks to Him. We don't need to be afraid that we will discard our faith or not prevail through the trial. We *will* persevere.

THE PARADOX OF JOY IN TRIALS

When we read that we are to consider it pure joy whenever we face our many trials, this joy is not a sigh of relief when the trial has ended. This is the paradox of joy in the midst of the trial.

Jesus experienced this paradox the whole time He was on earth. Jesus could never escape the knowledge that someday He would give His life on a cross for our sin. He agonized over lost people (Matt. 23:37) and openly wept when Lazarus died (John 11:35). Yet just hours before Jesus went to the cross, He said to His disciples, "I have told you this so that my joy may be in you and that your joy may be complete" (John 15:11).

Paul also experienced the paradox of joy in trials. He said he was "sorrowful, yet always rejoicing" (2 Cor. 6:10). He said, "I am greatly encouraged; in all our troubles my joy knows no bounds"

(2 Cor. 7:4). Paul was "rejoicing in hope, persevering in tribulation" (Rom. 12:12 NASB).

As Paul persevered through his trials, we know he didn't always feel happy about his circumstances. He said he was sorrowful. But does this mean the Apostle had lost his joy? No. Although Paul was sorrowful, he was also rejoicing. He said he experienced boundless joy in all of his many troubles.

Paul didn't pretend like the trial didn't hurt. He readily acknowledged his sorrow. Yet he also acknowledged the faithfulness of the Lord and His sufficiency to see him through the trials (2 Cor. 12:9). Paul rejoiced because the Lord gave him hope—a hope that enabled him to persevere through his trials with joy.

When we are passing through a painful trial and we're feeling unhappy or sorrowful, we may think our joy is gone. This is because we often confuse joy with circumstantial happiness. Jesus didn't feel happy about going to the cross, yet He spoke repeatedly about joy shortly before His death. Paul's circumstances were anything but happy, but his circumstances did not remove his joy.

It is normal for you and me to feel sorrow when a loved one dies, or if we discover we have a serious disease, or in any number of other things. When you and I feel sorrow, this doesn't mean we have lost our joy. What we have lost is our circumstantial happiness.

Joy is based on the unchanging truth of Jesus Christ's death and resurrection (1 Peter 1:3-5). No person or problem can change who He is and what He has done for us. Therefore, nothing can separate us from the joy we have in Him. Jesus said, "No one will take away your joy" (John 16:22).

When tribulation invades our lives, His promises don't change. He has redeemed us and called us by name. We belong to

Him. He is always with us.

As you and I go through our trials, do we believe God's promises? Do we believe He is in complete control? Do we believe He is faithful?

If we trust in the faithfulness of God as we face our trials, then we have joy. The reason we have joy is because we have faith. Joy and faith are intrinsically linked. Paul said, "Now may the God of hope fill you with all *joy* and peace *in believing* that you may abound in hope by the power of the Holy Spirit" (Rom. 15:13 NASB emphasis added).

If you are feeling distressed by the trial you are enduring, this doesn't mean you have lost your joy. Faith is the soil where the flowers of joy bloom. If you are trusting the Lord in the midst your trial, then the flowers of joy are blooming—even if your sorrow makes it hard to smell their fragrance.

In the winepress of affliction, as we trust in God's faithfulness to us, He places a hope and peace within us that passes human understanding. Though we may have tears on our face, we have joy in our hearts because we love God. And we know He loves us. We know that God is using the refining process to make us like His Son. And nothing is more important than becoming like Him (Rom. 8:29).

A PERSONAL STORY OF JOY

The paradox of joy in the midst of trials reminds me of an unexpected telephone call I received from my Mom several years ago. She was supposed to be on vacation, so at first I was puzzled by her call. "I didn't go on vacation," she said. "I'm having surgery this week."

The whole thing seemed so unreal. Leaving my family...driving to her home...the surgery...the waiting room...the news...highly unusual cancer...poor prognosis.

On Easter afternoon, my family drove to her home (where I was staying), and I made a big dinner for all of us. Mom seemed to be doing better that day, but her improvement didn't last. Later in the week she didn't even feel well enough for me to rub her back, so I just sat on the end of the bed.

That was when Mom told me she decided to not take any treatments for her cancer. I put my head down next to her on the pillow and cried. When she told me not to feel so sad, I said, "Mom, I grieve, but not as one who has no hope."

Although my circumstances were sorrowful, I knew the Lord knew all about this long ago. He is my faithful Friend and "the One who lifts up my head" (Ps. 3:3 NKJV). I comforted myself with the words of the psalmist who said, "I will be glad and rejoice in your love, for you saw my affliction and knew the anguish of my soul" (Ps. 31:7).

After Mom went to sleep that night, I stayed up and looked through some of her books. In the front of a book, I discovered something she had written. When I asked her about it the next morning, she said that a few months earlier she had been drawn to read verses in the Bible about joy in the midst of trials. Mom told me she began to pray that God would prepare her for whatever might lay ahead.

She wrote the words I found in the book the week before she learned she had cancer—during the time God was preparing her to face her trial with joy. This is what she wrote:

> Joy is like the cool refreshment of an ever-flowing mountain stream. My God continually washes away my tears of discouragement, disappointment, and heartache as He splashes His grace and peace over my troubled soul. He is my Rock. In the midst of deep waters, I

> will cling to Him. As I face each tomorrow, I will sing for joy as I take refuge in the shadow of His wings.

Mom lived less than four months after her initial diagnosis. In a weak, frail voice she whispered her final words to me: "See you in the morning."

If Mom could have said more, I'm sure she would have told me she was thinking about the verse that says, "Weeping may endure for a night, but joy comes in the morning" (Ps. 30:5 NKJV). The joy of the Lord strengthened her until the end—when she entered into the joy of His presence. Yes, I will see her and my Savior in the morning.

REAL JOY

The joy Jesus gives us is real. Joy isn't an abstract concept that floats away under pressure. When you and I go through real trials, *Jesus'* joy gives us real strength. "The joy of the Lord is your strength" (Neh. 8:10). Our joy is in *His* strength—in *His* ability to carry us through the trial. *He* enables us to persevere through tribulation. *His* joy deeply imbedded within us becomes our joy as we experience His strong hand holding us up and sustaining us.

His love and faithfulness are the bedrock that undergird us as we go though trying times. Tornadoes may tear through our lives, but deep within us His love and faithfulness remain unmoved. This is the solid foundation on which joy triumphantly stands.

Oswald Chambers said,

> The bedrock of Christian faith is the unmerited, fathomless marvel of the love of God exhibited on the Cross of Calvary, a love we never can and never shall merit....Undaunted radiance is not built on anything

> passing, but on the love of God that nothing can alter. The experiences of life, terrible or monotonous, are impotent to touch the love of God, which is in Christ Jesus our Lord.[1]

The harder the trial, the harder we lean against Jesus. His intimate presence strengthens us to persevere through our trials with joy, because we know our trials are not ours alone—they also belong to Him.

IN THE MIDST OF TRIALS, JOY IS . . .

Joy is . . . a supernatural response to adversity
produced by the Holy Spirit
the fruit of abiding in Christ.

Joy is . . . beyond earthly explanation
knowing this world isn't all there is
the anticipation of heaven.

Joy is . . . independent of circumstances
the offshoot of faith
beyond thieves.

Joy is . . . the presence of Jesus
the promises of His Word
the prospect of seeing Him.

Joy is . . . built on hope
fueled by faith
when all looks bleak.

Joy is . . . an emotional response to His love
believing He is in control
of every detail of my life.

Joy is . . . being redeemed and called by name
belonging to Him
remembering He is always with me.

Joy is . . . not found in what I see around me
but only and always
in Jesus.

Responding to God's Word

1. Read Hebrews 4:15-16. How do these verses encourage you?

2. How do the following verses help to comfort you in your present trial?

   Psalm 56:8

   Psalm 147:3

   Isaiah 41:10

   Isaiah 49:15-16

3. What does the wire brush of a trial accomplish? Can you think of a specific trial in which you saw this happen in the past, or currently see this happening?

4. What person in the Bible especially encourages you by the way he or she went through trials? Why? How can you follow his or her example?

5. Paul said he was "sorrowful, yet always rejoicing" (2 Cor. 6:10). Can you think of a time when you've experienced this? What did God teach you about Himself?

6. What does the Bible say to rejoice in?

   Psalm 32:11

   Habakkuk 3:17-19

   Philippians 4:4

   How does rejoicing in the Lord affect the way you go through your trials?

7. Read Psalm 33:21. How do you think faith and joy are intrinsically linked? What did you learn in this chapter about faith that encouraged you?

8. Read 1 Corinthians 10:13. How would you put this verse in your own words? What is the foundation of joy?

9. Describe what joy looks like in the midst of a trial. How does this help you persevere?

8

TRIALS: THE PATH TO INTIMACY WITH GOD

I woke up one morning filled with excitement as I anticipated my upcoming plans. I said to my husband, "Starting tomorrow morning, I'm going to spend the next two weeks at the computer working on my writing." Later on in the morning, I noticed some strange pains in my stomach. The pain didn't last long, so I forgot about it. Until evening. After dinner, I was suddenly hit with tremendous pain that kept me awake the whole night.

The next morning, I was not sitting at the computer as I had planned. I was sitting in the doctor's office and hearing him say, "You need to get to the hospital immediately for emergency surgery."

Later that day, as I was being wheeled down the hall to the operating room, I thought, *Lord, my life and my times are in Your hands*. Of course, I already knew this. But as I entered the glare of the bright lights of the operating room, this knowledge took on a new meaning. A meaning I wouldn't have experienced so deeply if I were sitting at the computer instead of lying on an operating table.

It's one thing to acknowledge that my life and times are in God's hands when everything is fine. It's a different story, however, when someone is about to stick me with a needle, and I know the last time I had a general anesthesia I reacted to a drug and nearly died. In that context, I clung to God's sovereign control over the details of my life with everything in me.

At home in bed, recovering from the operation, I realized this unexpected trial had taught me a valuable lesson. I came to see that if my plans had gone my way, I wouldn't have experienced the intimacy of the Lord's presence in such a deep way.

AN OPPORTUNITY FOR JOY

In the last chapter, we talked about facing our trials with joy because we know God is using trials to perfect our faith. In this chapter, we will learn how trials become the path to experiencing the joy of greater intimacy with the Lord.

In the New Living Translation, James 1:2-4 say, "Dear brothers and sisters, whenever trouble comes your way, let it be an *opportunity for joy*. For when your faith is tested, your endurance has a chance to grow. So let it grow, for when your endurance is fully developed, you will be strong in character and ready for anything" (emphasis added).

These verses describe trials as an opportunity for joy. How are trials an opportunity for joy?

- Trials give us the opportunity to experience the joy of the Lord's presence more intimately.

- Trials take the truth we know about God and push it deep within us.
- Trials make our intellectual knowledge of God experiential.

You and I could intellectually agree with the truth of James 1:2-4, but if we never went through any trials we wouldn't know, experientially, what this joy is. For example, let's say you tell me about your favorite place to eat. You describe in detail the delicious food, the great service, and how the restaurant is decorated. The best I can do is to imagine what you're talking about. But if I eat at the restaurant myself, I will know, experientially, what you mean.

Trials take what we know about God and make it a reality in our lives. If we had no trials, how could we experience the reality of God's faithfulness in trials? How could our faith mature if we had no testing to refine our faith? How could we know the intimacy of God's presence with us in trials if we had no trials?

One day our daughter, Whitney, walked into the kitchen saying, "I know God is in control of the details of my life." Whitney was going through a trial at the time, so she verbalized what she knew to be true about God.

I smiled at Whitney and said, "God is always in control of the details of our lives."

Whitney replied, "But when you're going through a trial, you think about it!"

Trials take what we know to be true about God and thrust it to the front of our minds. As we go through trials, we come to know the truth of God's Word at a deeper level. God is an intimate, personal God who wants us to know Him in an intimate, personal way. He desires to use our trials to turn us toward Himself and to reveal to us His intimate care and love. We will discover how God accomplishes this as we look at the trial Shadrach, Meshach, and Abednego faced.

A LITERAL FIERY TRIAL

Shadrach, Meshach, and Abednego were three Hebrew young men, probably teenagers, who were among the exiles who were captured and taken away to Babylon. Imagine what it was like for them to be ripped away from their homes and families and carried off to a foreign land. In a brainwashing attempt to strip them of their identity, their own names that honored God were taken away from them and replaced with names that honored pagan gods.

Hananiah, "Yahweh is gracious" became Shadrach, "Command of Aku." Mishael, "Who is what God is?" became Meshach, "Who is what Aku is?" Azaraiah, "Whom Yahweh helps" became "Abednego, "Servant of Nebo."

As if all this weren't bad enough, the crowning attempt to turn them into full-fledged Babylonians came when Shadrach, Meshach, and Abednego were commanded to fall down and worship a statue of a false god.

In the opening verses of Daniel 3, we discover that King Nebuchadnezzar made an image of gold (most likely a representation of himself) and demanded everyone to fall down and worship it. Shadrach, Meshach, and Abednego drew the line at that point. They had pagan names, but they would not worship a pagan god. They refused to worship anyone but the true God.

In Daniel 3:13-15, we read King Nebuchadnezzar's reaction to their refusal to worship the image:

> Furious with rage, Nebuchadnezzar summoned Shadrach, Meshach and Abednego. So these men were brought before the king, and Nebuchadnezzar said to

> them, "Is it true, Shadrach, Meshach and Abednego, that you do not serve my gods or worship the image of gold I have set up? Now when you hear the sound of the horn, flute, zither, lyre, harp, pipes and all kinds of music, if you are ready to fall down and worship the image I made, very good. But if you do not worship it, you will be thrown immediately into a blazing furnace. Then what god will be able to rescue you from my hand?"

All of us go through fiery trials that test our faith. Shadrach, Meshach, and Abednego faced a testing of their faith through a literal fiery trial that could cost their lives. How did they respond to King Nebuchadnezzar's threat?

> "O Nebuchadnezzar, we do not need to defend ourselves before you in this matter. If we are thrown into the blazing furnace, the God we serve is able to save us from it, and he will rescue us from your hand, O king. But even if he does not, we want you to know, O king, that we will not serve your gods or worship the image of gold you have set up" (vs. 16-18).

King Nebuchadnezzar became so furious that his face became contorted with rage. He immediately had Shadrach, Meshach, and Abednego bound and thrown into a furnace that was so hot, the men who threw them in were killed. Then something amazing happened:

> King Nebuchadnezzar leaped to his feet in amazement and asked his advisers, "Weren't there three men that we tied up and threw into the fire?" They replied, "Certainly, O king." He said, "Look! I see four men walking around in the fire, unbound and unharmed, and the fourth looks like a son of the gods." Nebuchadnezzar

> then approached the opening of the blazing furnace and shouted, "Shadrach, Meshach and Abednego, servants of the Most High God, come out! Come here!" (vs. 24-26).

Shadrach, Meshach, and Abednego emerged from the fire. Not a hair on their bodies was singed. Their clothes weren't scorched, and they bore no smell of smoke.

God delivered them out of the fire, alive and well. Shadrach, Meshach, and Abednego had boldly expressed their confidence that God was able to keep them alive. But even if He chose not to, they would still continue to trust in the Lord. They knew their lives and times were in the hands of the sovereign Lord who controls all things.

The faith of Shadrach, Meshach, and Abednego was not conditional on things going according to their plans. In the crucible—when they would have to choose whether to trust God or be thrown into the furnace—they placed their faith squarely in Him. They willingly submitted themselves to the Lord and His plans for their lives. They didn't bend their knees before the image just enough to save their lives. Shadrach, Meshach, and Abednego took an uncompromising stance of faith. Consequently, they were thrown into a fiery furnace.

THE JOY OF SEEING JESUS

While Shadrach, Meshach, and Abednego were in the fiery furnace, someone suddenly appeared with them. They saw someone, who King Nebuchadnezzar described as one who looked like "a son of the gods" (Dan. 3:25). Bible scholars believe this fourth man in the fire was most likely the preincarnate Christ. In the midst of their fiery trial, these three young men saw Jesus.

When you and I are in the midst of our fiery trials, we see Jesus! Not with our physical eyes, but with the eyes of our hearts.

Through faith, we see Him standing with us in our trials—comforting, strengthening, and encouraging us. In the heat of the trial, we experience the joy of His presence in a deeper way and come to know Him more intimately. Our joy in trials is seeing Jesus with us in the fiery furnace. Joy isn't the absence of trials; it's the presence of Jesus.

In his devotional book, *Morning and Evening Daily Readings,* Charles Spurgeon beautifully describes the believer's joy of seeing Jesus in the fiery trial:

> Blessed is the fact that Christians can rejoice even in the deepest distress; although trouble may surround them, they still sing; and, like many birds, they sing best in their cages. The waves may roll over them, but their souls soon rise to the surface and see the light of God's countenance; they have a buoyancy about them which keeps their head always above the water, and helps them to sing amid the tempest, "God is with me still."
>
> To whom shall the glory be given? Oh! To Jesus—it is all by Jesus. Trouble does not necessarily bring consolation with it to the believer, but the presence of the Son of God in the fiery furnace with him fills his heart with joy.[1]

You may be going through your present trial because Jesus loves you so much that He wants you to see Him and experience His care for you in a deeper way. Your trial is not an indicator of His indifference, but the opposite. He wants to use your trial to draw you closer to Him so you will know His tender love for you more intimately.

Jesus doesn't want you and me to know Him from a comfortable distance. He wants us to know Him up close. When things get uncomfortable in our lives, what do we do? We run to Jesus for comfort. Trials cause us to look at the Lord more intently and experience His comfort more intimately.

One summer night, I stepped onto our deck to gaze at the stars. But I couldn't see them because they were covered with clouds. I thought to myself, *Although I can't see the stars right now, I know they are still there. And sometimes, Lord, if I can't see You so clearly, I know You are still there.*

Just as the stars still shine on a cloudy night, through the eyes of faith, we see our Lord still seated on His throne as glorious as ever. When the clouds of trials roll into our lives, you and I are forced to look at the Lord more intently. If our lives consisted of all sunny days with no trials, He knows we wouldn't walk as closely with Him.

Because the Lord loves us and doesn't want us to miss the joy of an intimate relationship with Him, He uses trials to pull us close to Him. Trials cause us to focus on the Lord because we realize how much we need Him.

TRUSTING GOD WITH UNANSWERED QUESTIONS

As Shadrach, Meshach, and Abednego faced their trial of the fiery furnace, they expressed their complete confidence in God. They also admitted they didn't know for sure how their trial would end. God didn't tell them those details. Nevertheless, they trusted in Him and left the details in His hands.

The question we want answered when we're going through a trial is: how and when will it end? As in the case of Shadrach, Meshach, and Abednego, God generally chooses to not disclose that information to us. Although we know God is in control of the details of our lives, He doesn't reveal to us all the details of our lives. He doesn't give us all the answers to all of our questions.

Because God doesn't tell us everything we want to know, this doesn't mean He is indifferent or unconcerned. Do we tell our three-year-old child everything? No. We withhold certain information from him. But this doesn't mean we don't love him. We know there are certain things a child can't know or understand.

We are God's children, and God knows there are things we can't know or understand. But this doesn't mean He doesn't love us. God knows how weak we are and how we tend to rely on ourselves. If we knew all the answers to our questions and where every piece of the puzzle fit, we wouldn't trust Him as much. Because God loves us, He gives us only part of the picture, so we have to lean harder on Him. This builds the intimate relationship of love and dependency upon Him that He desires us to enjoy.

Although God may not show you where every piece of the puzzle fits, He holds all the pieces in His hands. And not one of them is missing. Will you trust Him with the pieces you can't see?

When we're facing a trial, we often spend much of our time and energy trying to understand what can't be understood and trying to unravel what God hasn't revealed. God wants us to trust in Him and what He has revealed to us in His Word. God doesn't tell us the whole story about our trial from beginning to end—even though He knows it. He tells us to trust Him. This is faith.

OPAL: A WOMAN OF JOY

Opal was a woman of faith who experienced the joy of the Lord's presence through a chronic trial. When I was a little girl, Opal, and her brother, Dave, were close friends of my family. Every Christmas, I could hardly wait for them to walk into my grandmother's house with boxes of presents and Opal's homemade cookies.

When Opal and Dave were older, they moved away. Opal spent her final years in a nursing home in Montana. She was limited to eating soft foods like mashed potatoes, and arthritis had disabled eight of her fingers. But with her two good fingers, Opal typed letters to me that included recipes for her delicious cookies, reviews of books and sermons, her perspective on world events, and proclamations like, "He is risen from the dead and coming again soon for His own! Hallelujah!!!"

Opal's faith and joy were cemented in the Lord. Her circumstances certainly gave her no reason to rejoice. Each day was a monotonous repetition of the previous day. Same bed. Same walls. Same food. If there were any changes at all, it was the addition of more pain.

One day when I read one her letters I thought, *I have feet that take me where I want to go. I have teeth that chew whatever I put into my mouth. I have ten working fingers. If I were in Opal's situation, would I be filled with such great joy?*

Since I want to finish strong like Opal, I wrote and asked her how she was able to keep going. She wrote back to me and said, "My dear, you already know the answer. My love for the dear Savior who you believe in and telling everyone I can to open their hearts to receive God's Word is what keeps me going."

The daily trial of living in a nursing home and failing health did not dampen Opal's faith and joy. Her earthly circumstances were dismal, but her joy was heavenly. Although Opal couldn't anticipate enjoyment from her circumstances, she anticipated the joy of the Lord's intimate presence with her from day-to-day.

Do you anticipate seeing Jesus with you in your trial? Do you view your trial as a path to experiencing greater intimacy with the Lord? Lean hard against Him and let Him hold you up. Let Him comfort you. Let Him be your joy and strength.

James said to "*let* endurance have its perfect result, that you may be perfect and complete, lacking in nothing" (1:4 NASB emphasis added). As we face our trials, we let God be God. We let God do His sovereign work of maturing our faith through the trials for His glory and our good.

Opal let the trial accomplish its work of making her more like Jesus as she persevered each day through her trial. In a nursing home, confined to a bed, Opal let the nearness of the Lord and His Word be her sustaining joy. The joy Opal experienced in her trial did not necessarily express itself as laughter and merriment. Her joy was a deep-seated peace and confidence of knowing God was in control of every detail of her life—even the details she couldn't see.

FIXING OUR EYES ON JESUS

As you and I face our trials, it helps to have an example to follow. Jesus provides our perfect example of One who persevered and triumphed through His trials. The writer of Hebrews said,

> Let us fix our eyes on Jesus, the author and perfecter of our faith, who for the joy set before him endured the cross, scorning its shame, and sat down at the right hand of the throne of God. Consider him who endured such opposition from sinful men, so that you will not grow weary and lose heart (12:2-3).

When you and I are going through a trial, we look to Jesus for our help and comfort. We fix our eyes on the Lord. We look at Him with a steadfast gaze.

When Shadrach, Meshach, and Abednego were in the fiery furnace, what would they have looked at? Jesus. In the midst of their trial, He was the focus of their gaze. Can we imagine them fixing their eyes on anything but Jesus?

To fix our eyes on Jesus means "to look away to Jesus." When we look away to Jesus, we look away from other things. What do we look away from? We look away from ourselves, away from our fear, away from our circumstances, away from Satan's lies, away from all else but Jesus.

All these voices scream at us, "Look at me!" Jesus calmly says to us, "Look at Me."

I have a flip calendar that has a quotation for each day. The page for September eighth says, "We need to learn that true Christianity is inseparable from deep joy; and the secret of that joy lies in a continual looking away from all else up to God, His love, His purpose, His will."[2]

As we go through our trials, we fix our eyes on Jesus, "the author and perfecter of our faith" (Heb. 12:2). He is the author of our faith because He began or originated our faith. He is also the perfecter of our faith because He matures our faith and brings it to completion.

When you and I face our many trials, we don't look to our faith to carry us through. We look to Jesus. Our faith is not in our faith. Our faith is in Jesus—the One who gave us our faith, sustains our faith, and perfects our faith. Faith is looking away from all else and trusting in Jesus alone.

Fixing our eyes on Jesus is like a child crossing the street with his daddy. When a little child crosses the street, does he worry about the traffic? No. He knows his daddy is holding his hand. The child doesn't fear the cars because he knows his daddy is watching out for him. The child simply looks at his daddy and trusts him to get him across the street. With a childlike faith in Jesus, we simply look at Him and believe that because He is holding our hand, He will get us across the street.

Charles Spurgeon said, "Look not so much to thy hand with which thou art grasping Christ, as to Christ; look not to thy hope, but to Jesus, the source of thy hope; look not to thy faith, but to

Jesus, the author and finisher of thy faith....Keep thine eye simply on Him."[3]

JESUS' FOCUS ON THE FATHER

When Jesus went through His wrenching trial of the cross, where did He look? Jesus always looked to His faithful Father. Because Jesus entrusted Himself to His Father and didn't look away from Him, Jesus endured through His trial.

But Jesus didn't just endure His trial. Listen again to what Hebrews 12:2 says, "For the joy set before him [he] endured the cross." Jesus persevered through His trial for the joy.

As James 1:2 says to consider it pure joy when we face many kinds of trials, Jesus endured His trial because He considered the joy. Jesus didn't consider the cross itself a joy. He despised the shame of dying a humiliating death at the hands of executioners who viewed Him as accursed by God. Yet as awful as the cross was, Jesus endured His trial for the joy set before Him.

What was Jesus' joy? His joy was in His coming "resurrection and the enthronement with his Father."[4] Just prior to going to the cross, Jesus expressed His longing to be reunited with the Father and to know the pleasure of being glorified with Him again in His presence. Jesus prayed, "And now Father, glorify me in your presence with the glory I had with you before the world began" (John 17:5). While Jesus was on earth, His glory was veiled by human flesh. Jesus endured the cross for the joy of once again being with the Father in unveiled, radiant glory.

Closely intertwined with Jesus' joy in His glory with the Father was His joy of saving us so we could see Him in His glory. Jesus looked forward to the joy of our being with Him in glory. In that same prayer, Jesus said, "Father, I want those you have given me to be with me where I am, and to see my glory, the glory you have given me because you loved me before the creation of the world" (John 17:24). Jesus anticipated the joy of us being with Him so we could gaze at His glory.

OUR FOCUS ON JESUS

As Jesus contemplated the cross, His joy was in His anticipation of once again being with the Father. As we face our trials, our joy is in our anticipation of someday being with Jesus. Right now, as we look at Jesus, we fix the spiritual eyes of our hearts on Him. But someday when we are in His presence, we will fix our physical eyes on Him. "They will see his face, and his name will be on their foreheads" (Rev. 22:4). We fix our eyes on Jesus now, in anticipation of our future joy.

Jesus endured the cross because He looked forward to the glorious day when He would again be in heaven and have the joy of us seeing Him in full, dazzling glory. We also look forward to this great day of joy when our eyes will gaze at the Lord. Job, in the midst of his many trials, also anticipated this same day of joy: "I myself will see him with my own eyes...How my heart yearns within me!" (Job 19:27). In heaven, we will have the joy of gazing at our glorious Savior forever.

As Jesus persevered through His trial for the joy set before Him, so we persevere through our trials with joy as we consider what He endured for us. Hebrews 12:3 says, "*Consider him* who endured such opposition from sinful men, so that you will not grow weary and lose heart" (emphasis added). When we consider the suffering He endured, we are strengthened and encouraged to not grow weary and lose heart. Jesus endured the suffering of His trial for the future joy, and we also endure the suffering of our trials for the future joy.

THE JOY OF A GREATER REALITY

Jesus endured the reality of the cross for the joy of a greater reality to come. As terrible as the cross was, its pain and shame were fleeting when compared to Jesus' joy of being in glory with His Father and with us. Jesus' trial was real, but He anticipated a greater reality to come. Jesus persevered through His trial because He looked away from what was seen to the joy of the greater, unseen reality.

Paul also had this same eternal perspective on his trials. He said, "Therefore we do not lose heart. Though outwardly we are wasting away, yet inwardly we are being renewed day by day. For our light and momentary troubles are achieving for us an eternal glory that far outweighs them all. *So we fix our eyes not on what is seen, but on what is unseen. For what is seen is temporary, but what is unseen is eternal*" (2 Cor. 4:16-18 TLB emphasis added).

When Paul referred to his trials as light and momentary, he wasn't saying his trials didn't matter. Paul went through many difficult trials. But the weight of glory to come is so exceedingly great, that *in comparison,* Paul said it made his trials look light and momentary. Paul didn't focus on what he could see around him. That would soon be over. Paul's joy was fixed on the eternal, unseen reality.

Like Paul, we focus on the greater reality of Christ seated on His throne in everlasting glory. Our trials are light and momentary *when compared* to the unending joy we will experience in the presence of the Lord.

Peter, writing to those who were suffering, also spoke of the brevity of trials when compared to eternal glory. "And the God of all grace, who called you to his eternal glory in Christ, after you have suffered a little while, will himself restore you and make you strong, firm and steadfast" (1 Peter 5:10). Our trials are temporary, but our joy is everlasting. We persevere through our trials for the joy of the greater, unseen reality.

THE GREATER REALITY: A PERSONAL STORY

When I focus on the unseen reality, it helps me to persevere through my trials with the right perspective. For example, one evening while I was using my lap top computer, it suddenly locked up. I frantically tried to access a file—any file, but I couldn't get into anything. My son performed some amazing feats on the computer and rescued one file, but that was all. The hard drive had crashed, and in a moment a year's worth of work disappeared.

The finality hit me. It was over. I felt numb as I slumped into a chair. The whole thing made no sense. But I knew that trying to figure out things I couldn't understand would not help me. I didn't allow myself to head down that pointless and discouraging road. What did help me was to say to myself, *This trial is a test. How am I going to respond to it?*

My thoughts began to turn toward the unseen reality, and I began to think about the angels in heaven. Since angels are created beings who don't know everything about God, one of the ways they learn about Him is by observing us. In 1 Corinthians 4:9, Paul talked about being a spectacle to both men and angels. I asked myself, *What are the angels learning about God as they watch me go through this trial?*

As I looked at my trial from an eternal perspective, I began to worship God for being the sovereign Lord who is in control of every detail of my life. I thanked Him for being kind and good. I praised Him for His love and faithfulness. As I was praying, I was filled with such joy to think that the angels might be falling down and worshiping God all the more for what they saw Him doing in me.

One day, a few weeks after the hard drive crashed, I decided to check what I had saved on our other computer. I found a file I hadn't thought about for a long time called *pathjoy*. Since I didn't have anything else to work on, I decided to develop *pathjoy*. This book, *The Path of Joy*, may not have been written if I hadn't lost everything first.

On the evening when the hard drive crashed, I had no way of knowing anything good would result from it. But if I never saw anything good come out of the trial, I knew God was still good. He still loved me. He was still in control. In the unseen realm, He was accomplishing His good purpose of refining my faith and making me more like Jesus.

Did you ever think you might be going through your trial so the angels will learn more about God's goodness and faithfulness? What are the angels learning about God as they observe how you go through your trials? When you go through trials that don't seem to make any earthly sense, don't discount what is happening in the heavenly realm.

HEAVEN: THE FINAL WORD ON TRIALS

God uses trials to turn our thoughts toward the greater, eternal reality of heaven. Our faith is firmly attached to the unseen reality of our future with Christ. God uses trials to prevent us from basing our hope on the shifting circumstances of this world. He wants us to base our hope on what is eternally unshakable.

The more difficult our trials, the more we look forward to heaven. Trials turn our thoughts toward Jesus. Adversity reminds us of the suffering He endured for us. Sorrow makes us long to see His face. The thought of being with Jesus produces a joy within our hearts unlike anything on earth. We could say our joy is out of this world!

Heaven has the final word on trials and suffering. Although Jesus suffered through an agonizing death, in a blaze of glory God raised Him from the dead (Acts 2:24). Although our trials may seem to never end, they will end someday. In a blaze of glory, God will raise us up to be with Him forever (2 Cor. 4:14). In heaven, Jesus Himself will personally welcome us home, saying, "Enter into the joy of your master" (Matt. 25:21 NASB).

In heaven, our trials will stop—finally and forever. These are some of the joys you and I can look forward to on the day when Jesus welcomes us home:

> He shall wipe away every tear from their eyes; and there shall no longer be any death; there shall no longer be any mourning, or crying, or pain; the first things have passed away (Rev. 21:4 NASB).

> The LORD will be your everlasting light, and your days of sorrow will end (Is. 60:20).

> Gladness and joy will overtake them, and sorrow and sighing will flee away (Is. 51:11).

Can you imagine being overwhelmed, overtaken with gladness and joy? In heaven, our joy will be so complete that not only will our sorrow cease, but we will never even sigh. This is the greater, unseen reality to come!

While you and I are in this world, we experience joy as we fix the eyes of our hearts on Jesus and hope in what we don't see: our future with Him. In heaven, we will have no more need of hope because we will be with Jesus and see Him with our own eyes. Our hope will end, but our joy will never end. "So we do not look at what we can see right now, the troubles all around us, but we look forward to the joys in heaven which we have not yet seen. The troubles will soon be over, but the joys to come will last forever" (2 Cor. 4:18 TLB).

The joy Jesus gives us now whets our appetite for the eternal joy to come. Right now, we experience the joy of His spiritual presence as we persevere through our trials. Then, we will experience the joy of being in His actual, physical presence. "You will fill me with joy in your presence, with eternal pleasures at your right hand" (Ps. 16:11).

In His presence, we will know the continual fullness of His joy and the bliss of His forever pleasures. While we don't know exactly what all these pleasures will be, I think if we were able to experience the fullness of such extreme delight in our mortal bodies of flesh, our hearts would literally explode!

A great and glorious day is coming when we will have the pleasure of enjoying an intimate relationship with Jesus in His presence forever. Until that day, He calls you and me to walk with Him along the path of joy as we anticipate the fulfillment of His promise:

> To him who is able to keep you from falling and to present you before his glorious presence without fault and with great joy—to the only God our Savior be glory, majesty, power and authority, through Jesus Christ our Lord, before all ages, now and forevermore! Amen (Jude 24-25).

Responding to God's Word

1. How are trials an opportunity to experience the joy of greater intimacy with God?

2. What do the following verses say about the Lord's sovereignty and intimate knowledge of you? How does this encourage you?

   Psalm 121:1-3

   Psalm 139:1-5

   Matthew 10:29-31

3. Imagine looking into the fiery furnace that Shadrach, Meshach, and Abednego faced. How were they able to stand strong and persevere? What do you see in them that you can apply to a fiery trial you may be facing?

4. How do trials cause you to look more intently at the Lord? How do you think God desires to use your trial to draw you closer to Himself?

5. Read Isaiah 40:26. How does this verse help you as you think about the "missing" pieces in your life? Why does God often choose to not reveal the whole picture? What do you think He desires you to learn about Him?

6. What was Opal's joy in the midst of her trial? How did she let her trial accomplish its perfect work? How does her example encourage you to let your trial finish its work?

7. What does it mean to fix your eyes on Jesus? How does this enable you to persevere?

8. What was Jesus' joy as He contemplated the cross? What is your joy as you face your trials?

9. Read 2 Corinthians 4:16-18. How does the joy of the greater unseen reality encourage you? How will a heavenly perspective of your trials, especially when they make no earthly sense, help to transform the way you go through them?

THE RELATIONSHIP YOU WERE CREATED TO ENJOY

When I read a magazine, I generally turn to the last page and read each article from last to first. And when I buy a book, I often turn to the last chapter to see how the author concludes the book. I don't like to wait to find out how everything ends.

None of us know when our lives will end, but we don't have to wait to find out where we will end up. God tells us: "You may know that you have eternal life" (1 John 5:13). Reading this verse is similar to reading the last page in a book. It tells us we can know we have eternal life, but how can we know? Let's start at the beginning and discover how we can receive eternal life, have all of our sins forgiven, and enter into a relationship of love with Jesus Christ.

The Problem

In the Bible, we read: "All things were created by him [Jesus Christ] and for him" (Col. 1:16). You and I were created by Jesus Christ for the purpose of glorifying Him and enjoying Him forever within the context of a loving, intimate relationship.

But there is a problem that prevents us from entering into this relationship with Jesus: sin. This problem isn't a subject people generally discuss over lunch. Sin may be uncomfortable for some of us to talk about. But if we have a disease, wouldn't we want to hear the truth about our condition? God compassionately tells us the truth about our sin disease so we will accept His cure.

God tells us: "All have sinned and fall short of the glory of God" (Rom. 3:23). This is a hard for many of us to accept. We don't feel particularly sinful. When we compare ourselves with other people, we see inconsistencies and mistakes in our lives, but we're reluctant to call it sin.

People aren't the standard of comparison. God is. When we compare ourselves with Him, if we're honest, we will admit we fall short of His righteousness. Just as one small hole is all it takes to ruin a piece of glass, one lie or one immoral thought is all it takes to prove we are sinners.

Since Adam first sinned, all of us have inherited a sinful nature that separates us from God. "Therefore, just as sin entered the world through one man, and death through sin, and in this way death came to all men, because all sinned" (Rom. 5:12). "Your iniquities have separated you from your God" (Is. 59:2). Our sin has created a huge gulf that separates us from the Lord and prevents us from enjoying a relationship with Him.

In an attempt to get across this chasm to God, maybe you've tried to live a good life or be religious. But our best efforts to reach

God are like trying to stretch a Band-Aid across the Grand Canyon. "All of us have become like one who is unclean, and all our righteous acts are like filthy rags" (Is. 64:6).

This news may be hard for some of us to accept. We don't think our condition is that bad. But God tells us our sin disease isn't just bad; it's fatal. "For the wages of sin is death" (Rom. 6:23). If we die without receiving the cure for our disease, we will be separated from God forever.

Some of us might assume that because God is loving, only the worst sinners go to hell. God is loving, and God is also just. His justice demands that all sin must be punished.

If a person commits a crime, he deserves to be punished. His crime places him in debt, and he must pay for what he has done. We have built up an insurmountable sin debt against God that we are powerless to pay. Yet God's justice demands it must be paid in full.

The Cure

God's love and justice intersected at the cross of Christ: "You see, at just the right time, when we were still powerless, Christ died for the ungodly....God demonstrates his own love for us in this: While we were still sinners, Christ died for us" (Rom. 5:6,8).

Because God couldn't overlook our guilt, He transferred our guilt onto Jesus Christ. "The LORD has laid on him the iniquity of us all" (Is. 53:6). Jesus paid in full the debt for our sin that we deserve to pay. He bore the death penalty for us. He took your place and mine on the cross when He was crucified to death.

"God made him who had no sin to be sin for us, so that in him we might become the righteousness of God" (2 Cor. 5:21). This verse tells us that because Jesus bore the punishment for our sin, God is able to release us from the punishment we deserve. He offers us the very righteousness of His Son and eternal life as a free, unmerited gift! "For the wages of sin is death, but the gift of God is eternal life in Christ Jesus our Lord" (Rom. 6:23).

Eternal life is not attained through good works, trying to be a good person, or by adding church traditions, rituals or *anything* to Jesus' sacrifice. Rather, we receive salvation as a free gift, apart from any added work, through faith in the work that Jesus did on the cross for us. Salvation is by faith alone in Christ alone. "For it is by grace you have been saved, through faith—and this not of yourselves, it is the gift of God—not by works, so that no one can boast" (Eph. 2:8-9).

After Jesus died, He didn't stay in the grave. "You, with the help of wicked men, put him to death by nailing him to the cross. But God raised him from the dead" (Acts 2:23,24). Because Jesus is alive, you can also be made spiritually alive and able to enjoy the relationship with Him for which you were created.

The sacrifice of Jesus was so comprehensive that God is ready, willing, and able to remove all your sins—past, present, and future. "Though your sins are like scarlet, they shall be as white as snow; though they are red as crimson, they shall be like wool" (Is. 1:18). Jesus Christ is the cure to your sin problem.

Your Response

If you were fatally ill and the doctor said your disease could be completely cured, would you accept His offer to cure you? If you chose not to accept his cure, you would die. If you decide not to accept God's cure for your sin, you will die in your sin and bear the punishment yourself (2 Thess. 1:9).

God offers you eternal life and forgiveness of all your sins. Will you receive His cure? To accept His offer to cure you of your sinful condition:

- *Agree* with what God says about your sin. Admit you are a sinner and that you have sinned against Him. Repent, or turn away from your sins. "Repent and believe the good news!" (Mark 1:15). You can't receive the cure if you won't let go of your disease.

- *Believe* that Jesus died on the cross in *your* place and rose again, and that He is the only way of salvation. "Salvation is found in no one else, for there is no other name under heaven given to men by which we must be saved" (Acts 4:12).

- *Surrender* control of your life to Jesus and obey Him as the Lord of your life and Savior from your sin. Jesus said, "Come, follow me" (Matt. 4:19).

I would like to give you the opportunity to respond to the Lord through prayer. You don't receive forgiveness and eternal life by saying a prayer, but through faith in Jesus Christ. Prayer is how we communicate with Him. To surrender your life to Jesus, sincerely pray the following prayer:

> "Lord, I admit that I have lived for myself and sinned against you in my thoughts, words, and actions. Thank you, Jesus, for taking the punishment for my sin that I deserve to pay. Right now, I'm turning away from my self-ruled life to follow You. Please forgive me of all my sin and give me eternal life. From today on, I'm yours."

As you begin your new relationship with Jesus:

- Learn about the Lord and grow in your relationship with Him through reading and studying the Bible. "Like new-born babes, long for the pure milk of the word, that by it you may grow" (1 Peter 2:2 NASB).

- Talk with the Lord through prayer. "Devote yourselves to prayer" (Col. 4:2).

- Regularly meet with other believers at a church where the Bible is taught. "Let us not give up meeting together" (Heb. 10:25).

- Tell others about your new relationship with Jesus. "Tell them how much the Lord has done for you, and how he has had mercy on you" (Mark 5:19).

NOTES

Introduction—A Childlike Joy

1. Thomas O. Chisholm, William M. Runyan, *Great Is Thy Faithfulness*, (Hope Publishing Company, 1923).

Chapter 1—Happiness and Joy

1. Dianne Hales, "How Teenagers See Themselves," *Chicago Tribune Parade Magazine*, Aug. 18, 1996, 5.

2. Philip Berman, "Search For Meaning," *Chicago Tribune Parade Magazine*, April 7, 1996, 21.

3. John MacArthur, *Joy and Godliness*, (Panorama City, CA: Grace to You, 1990), 8.

Chapter 2—Lost and Found: The Joy of Salvation

1. Martyn Lloyd-Jones, *The Life of Joy*, (Grand Rapids, MI: Baker Book House, 1989), 39, 40.

2. J. Oswald Sanders, *Enjoying Intimacy With God*, (Grand Rapids, MI: Discovery House Publishers, 2000), 43.

3. John Newton, *Amazing Grace! How Sweet the Sound*, 1779, Public Domain.

Chapter 3—The Joy of Knowing God

1. "The Best and Worst," *Chicago Tribune Parade Magazine*, Dec. 29, 1996, 12.

2. John MacArthur, *God Coming Face to Face With His Majesty*, (Wheaton, IL: Victor Books, 1993), back cover.

3. Martyn Lloyd-Jones, *Enjoying the Presence of God*, (Ann Arbor, MI: Servant Publications, 1993), 38.

4. Ibid, back cover.

5. J. Oswald Sanders, *Enjoying Intimacy With God*, (Grand Rapids, MI: Discovery House Publishers, 2000), 87,88.

6. A.W. Tozer, *The Knowledge of the Holy*, (San Francisco, CA: Harper & Row, Publishers, 1961), 3.

7. J. Oswald Sanders, *Enjoying Intimacy With God*, (Grand Rapids, MI: Discovery House Publishers, 2000), 90.

8. Charles Spurgeon, *The Fullness of Joy*, (New Kensington, PA: Whitaker House, 1997), 81.

9. Arthur Bennett, editor, *The Valley of Vision: A Collection of Puritan Prayers and Devotions*, (Carlisle, PA: The Banner of Truth Trust, 1994), 127.

Chapter 4—The Joy of Abiding in Christ

1. Bruce Wilkinson, *Secrets of the Vine,* (Sisters, OR: Multnomah Press, 2001), 18,19.

2. Andrew Murray, *The Secret of Spiritual Strength,* (New Kensington, PA: Whitaker House, 1997), 26.

3. J. Oswald Sanders, *Enjoying Intimacy With God,* (Grand Rapids, MI: Discovery House Publishers, 2000), 63.

4. Bruce Wilkinson, *Secrets of the Vine,* (Sisters, OR: Multnomah Press, 2001), 103.

5. Charles Spurgeon, *The Fullness of Joy,* (New Kensington, PA: Whitaker House, 1997), 94.

6. Oswald Chambers, *The Best From All His Books,* (Nashville, TN: Oliver-Nelson Books, 1987), 2.

7. Andrew Murray, *The Secret of Spiritual Strength,* (New Kensington, PA: Whitaker House, 1997), 34.

8. Martyn Lloyd-Jones, *Enjoying the Presence of God,* (Ann Arbor, MI: Servant Publications, 1991), 133.

Chapter 5—The Fruit of Joy

1. Martyn Lloyd-Jones, *Spiritual Depression Its Causes and Its Cure,* (Grand Rapids, MI: Eerdmans Printing Co., 1994), 297,300.

2. Oswald Chambers, *The Best From All His Books,* (Nashville, TN: Oliver-Nelson Books, 1987), 190.

3. Charles Spurgeon, *The Fullness of Joy,* (New Kensington, PA: Whitaker House, 1997), 87,88.

4. Oswald Chambers, *The Best From All His Books*, (Nashville, TN: Oliver-Nelson Books, 1987), 228.

5. R.C.H. Lenski, *The Interpretation of St. Paul's Epistles to the Galatians, Ephesians and Philippians*, (Minneapolis, MN: Augsburg Publishing House, 1961), 291.

6. Ibid, 619.

Chapter 6—The Joy of a Satisfied Soul

1. Joseph Stowell, *Perilous Pursuits*, (Chicago, IL: Moody Press, 1994), 126.

2. Isaac Watts, *When I Survey the Wondrous Cross*, 1707, Public Domain.

3. Oswald Chambers, *My Utmost for His Highest*, (Westwood, NJ: Barbour and Company, Inc., 1963), 1.

4. John F. Walvoord and Roy B. Zuck, *The Bible Knowledge Commentary*, (Colorado Springs, CO: Victor Books, 1983), 1132.

5. Martyn Lloyd-Jones, *Enjoying the Presence of God*, (Ann Arbor, MI: Servant Publications, 1991), 98.

6. A.W. Tozer, *The Pursuit of God*, (Camp Hill, PA: Christian Publications, 1993), 19, 20.

Chapter 7—Joy in the Midst of Trials

1. Oswald Chambers, *My Utmost For His Highest*, (Westwood, NJ: Barbour and Company, Inc., 1963), 48.

Chapter 8—Trials: The Path to Intimacy With God

1. Charles Spurgeon, *Morning and Evening Daily Readings*, (Grand Rapids, MI: Zondervan Publishing House, 1955), 368.

2. Mary Wilder Tileston, editor, quote by Charles Gore, *Joy and Strength*, (Bloomington, MN: World Wide Publications).

3. Charles Spurgeon, *Morning and Evening Daily Readings*, (Grand Rapids, MI: Zondervan Publishing House, 1955), 360.

4. R.C.H. Lenski, *The Interpretation of the Epistle to the Hebrews and the Epistle of James*, (Minneapolis, MN: Augsburg Publishing House, 1966), 428.

SCRIPTURE INDEX

PSALMS

PSALMS (cont'd)

PROVERBS

ECCLESIASTES

OUR GOAL

We believe God's people hunger to experience Him in a genuine, life transforming, and ever deepening way. This hunger is not satisfied with a formulaic approach to life, a theology that remains detached from life, or with experiences that lack scriptural grounding.

Rather, we believe God satisfies the longings of His people through a set of intimate relationships: with Himself through His Word and with His people.

Leadership Resources desires to bring believers into an encounter with God who is exalted in holiness, sovereignty, glory, and grace. We do this through in-depth teaching of His life giving Word that encourages, cleanses, and transforms His people. We seek to deepen commitments within a local body of believers and encourage restoration of damaged relationships. We seek to instill a renewed passion for God so all the earth might be filled with His glory.

LEADERSHIP RESOURCES INTERNATIONAL

Leadership Resources is a ministry of discipleship for churches and church leaders. We provide conferences, leadership training and materials designed to assist churches in the work of equipping their people for ministry. Our conferences in the area of discipleship, ministry, family, relationships and Inductive Bible Study are available to churches and mission organizations throughout the world.

The materials we produce are designed for personal use, one–to–one discipleship, Sunday School classes, home Bible studies and family ministries. Some of our studies are also published in Spanish.

For more information about our conferences or materials, contact:

Leadership Resources
12575 South Ridgeland Avenue
Palos Heights, IL 60463
(800) 980–2226

LRI@Leadershipresources.org